Face Reading

How to F̶ ̶ ̶ ̶ ̶ ̶e at a Glance

berts

© Copyright Barbara Roberts 2011. All rights reserved. No part of this manual may be reproduced in any manner, stored, or transmitted in any form or by any means: electronic, mechanical or otherwise, including photocopy, recording or any information storage and retrieval system without my written permission.

Barbara Roberts
Healing and Insight Publishers
1106 Second St., Suite #227 • Encinitas, CA 92024 • (760) 479-0008
Website: www.facereadingl.com

ISBN # 978-0-615-29798-9
Registered Library of Congress: July, 2009
Second edition, January 2013. Printed in United States.

TABLE OF CONTENTS

> *George Washington Carver created 200 products from the peanut. When asked how he did this he replied, "If you love something enough, it will share with you all its secrets."*

Tyra Banks wrote Barbara:

I loved having you on my talk shows, and definitely applaud and thank you for taking a similar stand to honor ethnic diversity in all ways in your work.

Dear Friends,   January, 2013

Your face tells the story of your life. Like a tracker in the Old West, everything is there for someone who knows how to look. Who we are is recorded in our body as our facial features. The purpose of this book is to give accurate, specific psychological meanings for each facial feature, which when applied to someone with that feature, will help us to better understand them.

We look at others without really seeing them. After reading this book, you will see them. Others, who before would have been strangers to you, now become very knowable.

When I first became interested in Face Reading in 1985, I read the 200 books on the topic. It was confusing to me that the psychological meanings for the same facial feature could be opposite in different books. Like a mole on the tip of the nose – half of the books said it meant "bankruptcy." The other half said it meant "financial abundance." It couldn't be both! So using my training in clinical medical research (UCSD), I sought to develop an accurate and repeatable system of psychological meanings which would honor people of all ethnic groups, ages and genders. In studying 10,000 faces, teaching 400 Classes, and working with live studio audiences in some 75 national/local TV Shows, people have validated each of these psychological meanings to be accurate for them, their co-workers, and families. My idea was to design a workbook-manual instead of a narrative book on face reading. This will allow you, the reader, to be able to open this book anywhere to look up the features of your spouse, mother-in-law, daughter, or boss.

As you develop your accuracy with these psychological-visual assessment skills, may your heart open to understand the underlying factors which make people behave in the ways they do. And with this may you feel compassion and gentleness in how you approach yourself and others.

My many thanks to Margaret whose encouragement and computer help made this book possible. Thanks to Robbie whose editing and photo finding was a great asset. And to my sister whose spiritual support has helped me throughout. And thank you to all my many friends who contributed photos and your time: Fran, Tasha, Bella, Mike, Aaron, Blake and Marisa, Jane, and the Lou Rubin family. And a heartfelt, special thanks to Jeff Calcara who went above and beyond to format and upgrade the text copy of this book!

Blessings to you and your family,

QUESTIONS AND ANSWERS
INTERVIEW WITH BARBARA ROBERTS

How did you become interested in Face Reading?

When I met my first teacher, a world famous psychologist and face reader, my personality was very scientific and logical. The concept of reading someone's face was "pretty out there" for me. He opened his class by asking if anyone wanted their face read. I popped up my hand and noticed no one else was volunteering. I wondered what I was getting myself into. He proceeded to tell me twenty things about my life all of which were 100% accurate. He went on to do this with everyone in the room.

Later, I showed him a photo of my father. His immediate response was, "Your father was an orphan, wasn't he?" True. Then, he went on to analyze my dad's smiling, slit shaped eyes (an unusual feature found in people who have emotionally pulled back for one reason or another). He gave details of how dad's challenge to form emotional connections was reflected in my own facial features and how I could heal this. His personal insights helped me to heal my relationship with my father before he died. I thought, "Whatever this man knows, I want to know it!"

After studying with him for a few years, he gave me his blessing to carry on his work and to teach it. My own face is narrow, the psychological meaning of which is "gifted but shy." The thought of teaching made me want to hide behind the sofa.

What did your (Midwestern) family think of you doing Face Reading?

The first time I was on NBC Nightly News, my twin brother, a well known Internist, called me to say, "What are you doing?!!" My conservative upbringing made me cringe when he made the sound "OO-EE-OO" from the Twilight Zone. I thought that the concept of California (my home) as the land of "fruits and nuts" was confirmed again in his brain.

Last Fall at his home in Illinois, he had a party for the doctors and staff from his clinic. I asked him what he wanted me to tell them I did for a living if they asked. (I didn't want to embarrass him). He said, "It's all right. They've read your book. And I don't care what you tell them about them, but when they go, I want to hear everything!"

And at the party, doctors and staff enthusiastically lined up to ask me to face read photos of their kids.

What do you look for when you first look at someone's face?

You look for the first five features that are the most prominent. It might be the fine, blonde hair, or hazel eyes, or long earlobes, or a tiny mouth. In my system everything means something psychologically. You interpret the features you see.

When an emotional tendency is strong in the character, it will appear in many areas of the person's face. Conversely, if a feature (perhaps with a negative meaning) shows only once, you ignore that feature. Hitler, for example, had many consistent features: a patch mustache (the meaning of which is paranoid and full of rage,) very small ears (the meaning of which is narcissistic and dangerous,) and an eye tone which was cold and cruel.

What about ethnic features? How do you read those?

When I see an African-American, Asian or Hispanic person, I assume they will have brown (black) hair and brown eyes as those are features which are common for someone of those ethnic backgrounds. (However, once I saw blue eyes in a man from Calcutta, a feature that was significant in the reading because it is so rare.) So, I ignore any features that might be related to an ethnic background and look for facial features that make that person spiritually and emotionally special. The goal is to go beyond the superficial and discover the deeper person inside.

What about plastic surgery? Botox?

Facial features fall into three types:

1) Features which appear at birth. Examples might be: long ear lobes, a high forehead, close set eyes or a thin upper lip, or hazel eyes.

2) Features which reflect how a person likes to look. This could be changing one's hair color from brown to blonde. Or when I teach at Macy's I refer to #2s as the whole bottom floor of Clinique, MAC, Revlon. This category reflects a person's spirit.

3) Features changed due to accidents, surgeries, melanoma, orthodontia. These reflect outside influences that alter one's appearance. (Plastic surgery would be #3).

What if you can't identify which one of the foreheads or lips . . . or ears the person has in this book?

Then, I usually ignore the area of his face which is unclear (a forehead that appears both square and round at the same time) and start on another part of his face – knowing that the underlying personality will express everywhere. And some facial features are harder to assess than others. (i.e. brown hair – a clear feature vs. small ears – not as obvious as it has to be measured) The more unusual a feature, the more accurate its psychological meaning.

Have you ever seen a face of someone who scared you?

Once at a large party I was reading guests as some of my students sat nearby. What I told the first seven people about their lives was 100% accurate. Then a man sat down with his girlfriend (a student of mine) cuddled next to him. She, of course, wanted to hear a glowing report of their compatibility. As I started the reading, nothing I said was accurate for him. He had grown up in the inner city of New York as part of a gang, (I heard later) but when I told him that, he denied it. So, I inwardly asked for clarity. The word "Mafia" came across my inner sight. There was no way I would put myself or my students' safety at risk! I looked at him and said, "You know, I don't seem to be able to do this for you. I'm sorry. Please accept your money back." He was stunned. The readings for the last seven guests were again 100% accurate.

A very unusual session involved Denise, a student from the class on Romance and Relationships, who had invited her fiancée so we could read their compatibility. As he entered the room, I saw his unusual ear shapes, severe scarring across the cheeks, his vacant gaze, unibrow and tiny mouth. My first thought was, "I'm the teacher. It's my role to keep this class safe."

I did what I call a "Teflon" reading – where I talk in generalities and say nothing either positive or negative. After the couple left, everyone mobbed

me in the parking lot, "What were you doing? You didn't say anything?!"

Later I called Denise and gave her my not-so-positive opinion about this romantic match for her, encouraging her to back out or at least take her time before committing to him.

"Well, he has had major concussions and brain surgery," she confided. "And he is on Haldol (a medication for psychosis), but I love him. I want to marry him."

I forgot about this until eight years later when I received a phone call from Arkansas.

"You might not remember me," Denise began. "But I wanted to tell you what happened. I married him, and we're in Arkansas at the prison. He tried to strangle me and kill my daughter. You were so right."

I was so sorry to hear her news. Being right isn't always so wonderful.

You talk about intuition. How is this helpful in Face Reading? And how does one develop it?

There are two parts of Face Reading. The first part I call the "science" of Face Reading – every facial feature has psychological meaning(s). That's cut and dried. You identify specific visual features on someone's face, and then (using this book), you look up the meaning(s). With that skill alone you can be 85-95% accurate in reading a person's character.

However, a much deeper level of Face Reading involves what I call "weaving," which is putting together multiple individual facial features to make a whole character analysis. This involves intuition, which I call the "art" of looking at someone. To develop this one focuses on seeing with the heart. As Le Petit Prince said, "Only with the heart can one see clearly."

I call this inner sight, because it goes deep into the unseen and reveals insights about the person's life situation. To be correctly aligned to this, one's focus must be on giving healing and insight, not criticism or judgment.

Intuition is a skill anyone can develop. Every successful person uses it consciously or unconsciously. My favorite story illustrating this is from the Bible. Baby Jesus is brought into the Temple by Mary and Joseph. A blind, old Jewish man proclaims the baby as the Messiah from his inner sight.

How is intuition different from imagination or having a strong opinion about someone?

First, with real intuition, "The proof is in the pudding." In other words, when you tell someone something specific, they nod and tell you that your perception is accurate for their life. Intuition is not speculative or vague.

The way I know the psychological meanings in this book are accurate is that thousands of people have sat in front of me validating them. During a session I frequently stop to ask a client "Is this true about you?"

If your words reflect true intuition, they bear "good fruit" – meaning they reflect truth – whether the topic for the person is negative or positive.

Also, with true intuition the person doing the reading feels a definite, deep feeling of peace moving through his heart and mind. There is an actual, physical experience of a subtle, positive, and peaceful energetic feeling that moves across the heart.

When combining individual facial features to make an accurate character reading of a client, sometimes I'll see what I describe as a crab shape: Facts about the person are at the center and the intuitions come out (like little legs). If the facts are true, then the intuitions that follow are also true.

In looking at others, it is important to be aware of and let go of any mental prejudices or negative judgements we have about them. This doesn't mean that we don't have discrimination about good vs. evil, but it does mean that we are open to listening to who others are.

A simple example: Let's say your face reading client has just put his beloved dog to sleep, and you are a cat lover. And when you were a child, you were bitten by a fierce dog. So when the person starts grieving about his dog, you could go into an emotional reaction based on your traumatic past experiences and verbally shut him down

OR you could strive to be aware of your inner dislike of dogs but be present and open to his grieving process.

If you find that when listening to someone, you get stirred up emotionally or feel dramatic intensity, stop before you speak. An emotional-dramatic response might not be useful or healing to the person.

The quickest way to develop accurate intuition is to meditate and/or do deep prayer work. In expanding our consciousness, we let go of our little ego and pettiness. We put our intention to be of service before God. Our intention is to give healing and insight. We attune to our quiet, inner stillness. Then we are really open to perceiving clearly the nature of the person before us.

When you talk about God, I'm completely turned off. Can I still become good at developing intuition and without being religious?

What I've noticed in my 20 years doing this is that there is a big difference between being spiritual and being religious. Some folks are spiritual yet never go to church. They have a deep love and understanding of family, friends, and humanity. They treat people with incredible care and compassion. My twin brother and his wife are like this. Others commune with nature or feel joy as they watch a baby laugh.

Hopefully someone who is religious also has a personal relationship with God. However, sometimes we hear of historical examples like the Inquisition where religious leaders killed for Christ or terrorists who kill for a religious cause. When I was in my 20s I lived for a short time in Belfast, Ireland, with a family whose mother was Catholic and father was Protestant. Every night we would watch the local TV news report of the street fighting and see all the deaths that occurred in the name of religion.

To develop intuition all one needs is a kind heart and the sincere desire to want to understand others.

From the thousands of faces I have read, below are some examples of interesting people, with details about their lives. Some of the insights come directly from understanding the psychological meanings for each facial feature. Other insights come from intuition.

Oprah's Producers

One morning I was a guest on a local TV News show, and one of the Oprah producers was present. After the segment, he took me aside and asked if I would read the faces of Oprah's staff from video clips he had with him.

He lamented, "There's one person we're having trouble with. She doesn't get along with anyone else, and it's very stressful. Can you see who it is?"

He nodded as I verbally went through each producer's face and management style. Then I stopped at Deborah, the person causing the problem. I said, "Others see her as a tyrant. She's very dominant. And I think in a year Oprah will take her off the Show."

"Deborah is Oprah's best friend," he countered. "Oprah would never fire her or let her go. She's going to be there after we all leave!"

A year later on the cover of TV Guide, I gazed at Deborah's photo. Caption read: "Oprah fires her best friend. Staff sees her as 'tyrant.' She gets two million dollar severance package."

The Future of a President

The day Bill Clinton was sworn in as president I appeared on the Morning News to analyze his face and predict the tone of his presidency.

"So what kind of president will he be?" the News anchor leaned in.

At the time America was looking for a "Kennedy" – a dynamic, charismatic leader. Popular presidents who had huge, strong jaws (Washington, Kennedy, and

FDR) were politicians known for their far reaching accomplishments. As Greek philosopher Aristotle hand-selected generals for Alexander the Great, he looked for this large jaw structure. And Alexander won dominion over the whole world.

But Clinton, whose face is round at the bottom, was going to have a softer, democratic style. Then I noticed the right and left sides of his face. His right side (which reflects his work life as President) was completely different from his left side (which reflects his personal and spiritual development). His right side was intelligent, articulate, and confident – so much so that there was even a smirk in the upper lip. The left side, however, was cold and manipulative. When I pointed this out in the studio, the whole TV crew gasped.

I predicted, "I believe that at some point in his presidency, Clinton will try to manipulate the American public, and the whole country will turn on him. And he won't like it."

Enter years later Monica Lewinsky.

"All is not as it appears"

In another session at my house, Massie walked into my office and turned to her 40 year old Japanese friend who looked very worried and tired.

"Barbara will know. You'll see. It'll be OK."

The woman produced a photo of her husband of twelve years.

"He's the head minister of a huge church. No one believes me," she sobbed.

I took the photo and covered the right side, then the left side of his face. The feeling coming from his right side (his work life as a famous minister) was confident and determined. However, the left side (his personal life with his wife and children) was completely different – cruel, brutal, and calculating.

"He's hurting you and the kids, isn't he?" I asked.

She nodded. "Yes. And no one sees it." she cried. "Everyone thinks he's so wonderful, and the children have welts on their backs from him beating them." We spent the next hour talking about her getting psychological help for her and the children.

He was a street angel and a home devil.

Secrets

"My husband, Jake, is lazy. He's not earning enough money to support us. He does . . ." and Lacey continued for 20 minutes criticizing her husband. When I took his photo, I saw a man who looked sad and work worn, but was not otherwise negative. Pondering his face as she spoke, I looked up to see her glazy focus, the wide area on the outside of her eyes (indicating a person who would overindulge in the senses) and her tiny ears. Not all her 'cards' were on the table and the 'excess' in her face had something to do with drugs and alcohol. I felt an intuition move across my heart in the calm, peaceful way it does when something is accurate.

"I hear that you wish to leave Jake. However, will leaving him solve your cocaine addiction?"

Her mouth dropped open and her eyes bugged out, "How did you know I'm a cocaine addict?" she stammered.

I said, "The same way I know..." and I continued to outline other aspects of her life as she nodded slowly. Then we spoke about her starting Narcotics Anonymous (a 12-step program) to work on her drug habit, which she thought was "hidden."

An Upscale Hair Salon

The red and green ornaments for Christmas were scattered throughout the large room. Festive music played, and chocolate desserts were laid out on long tables. But no one was moving. Forty people gathered behind me to listen as I read one face after another. Laughing, good humored snickers and some applause resounded behind me.

An older gentleman sat down, and I focused on his big money nose, bushy eyebrows, and determined chin. Definitely an entrepreneur! A man whose nose told me he was very wealthy. I went with my intuitive hunch, "John, do you have any connection with the word 'franchise'?"

Uproarious laughter surrounded me in stereo.

"I guess that means 'Yes?'" my eyebrows went up.

His wife turned to me, "He owns 80 franchises."

Blessings of a Saint

An older woman sat down quietly on the edge of a chair. It was a crowded room with a cloud of smoke and loud talking, so I could barely hear her voice. Her radiant eyes, clear and deep, revealed a spiritual seeker. Full cheeks showed deep feeling, and her bone structure was narrow and delicate. All these features showed she was deeply religious and devotional. As we spoke, my intuition became alert and I perceived the presence of a saint next to her.

"Do you have any connection with Padre Pio?" I asked.

"Padre Pio!!" she stammered in a thick Italian accent. "Why he baptized my mother and father and healed my brother! I grew up in the town where he lived. I love him!"

"He's here blessing you," I smiled.

We sat and devotionally shared the moment of his sacred presence.

A Controller

My student Shannon introduced her friend, Rachel, an energetic and dynamic woman who took a seat across from me.

"You know, Barb, I'm sort of skeptic of all this stuff."

Her face, blue-gray eyes and a narrow nose bridge, the combination suggesting a person who is analytical in a left-brained way. Someone who had deep concentration. Her close-set eyes reflected her ease at handling details. Great for an accountant or CPA. I put aside these perceptions as I proceeded to accurately describe her personality. Then a word came to me and I asked, "Are you a 'controller'? And I don't mean emotional."

"Why yes!" She was startled.

"Well, I don't know what that word means as I work in medicine. What is a controller?" I asked.

"It's the head of finance. I run a local casino," her mouth was agape.

Then behind her head I saw '80.' "Do you have 80 cashiers now?"

"Yes! How did you know?!" she was incredulous.

"And are four to five leaving?"

"Yes, they are!"

So I continued, "What you're really here about is…."

And she nodded as I outlined the questions on the paper in her lap.

A Missing Piece of the Puzzle

Rosa, a twenty-seven-year-old Hispanic nurse, made herself comfortable on my sofa. She started, "You saw me two years ago and told me that I would be married within a year – even though I wasn't dating anyone at the time. Then you told me I would have a little baby girl a year later. I did marry within that year, and a year later to the day my daughter Elena was born. You even told me that there would be some drama on the day of my wedding, and that came true, too!"

She continued, "What I don't understand though is that you also told me the little boy my husband and I want would come three to four years after the birth of the baby girl. Why is the second birth so far after my daughter's birth?"

I prayed and focused but nothing came. "I don't know," I shrugged. "I don't get anything."

Two months later her sister phoned me to say that Rosa was in the hospital having open heart surgery and dialysis after a major heart attack. Doctors told her that her recuperation from this devastating illness would take at least a year or more. Perhaps that is why the birth of a little boy will actually come later . . . maybe in three or four years? We'll see.

Double Identity

In Elizabeth's cozy ocean front home, her husband Ralph was making himself a turkey sandwich from the table laden with food for the women's group. Noticing his glasses, beard, mustache, and unusual ear shapes, he seemed secretive in a way I couldn't quite pinpoint. I continued doing the face readings of the women in front of me as a vague thought registered in my mind that "something wasn't right" in this home.

After leaving the party, I realized I had forgotten to give Elizabeth an address she wanted. Looking for her phone number, I realized I had accidentally thrown that paper away.

"It's OK," I thought, "I'll just look them up in the phone book."

The name was unusual, and the town small. A man answered the phone, and I asked for Elizabeth.

"There's no one by that name here," the man responded.

"But isn't this the Ralph B . . . residence in . . ." I was confused.

"Well, actually, it is, and I am Ralph B . . . However, the family you are seeking is not listed. I've been trying to find them for 10 years as the other 'Ralph' stole my identity. He continues to bill large amounts to my credit cards. He even named his children after my children! He's been wanted for years by the FBI."

Goebel's Ears

"Here's the photo of my brother-in-law. Can you tell me anything about him? I didn't know him very well." Louise handed me a black and white photo from the 1930's. A man in a three piece suit stood in front of a mahogany desk. Short haired and official looking. I took a closer look. His ears were the same shape as Goebel's (an officer from Hitler's men in World War II.) Though I usually aim to begin a session with positive statements, the following came out of my mouth, "So when did he go to prison?"

Her head jerked back and she breathed in slowly, "Right after this photo, and we never heard from him again."

"The truth will out"

My friend James rested against the hard back chair in my office. "I have someone's photo I want you to tell me about, Barb."

The man facing me in the photo wore a tattered, dirty T-shirt, as he leaned into a broken lawn chair. The overgrown grass behind him was brown and jagged. His face had a three-day-old beard. Then I saw the biggest large nose I had ever seen and knew what was up. "He's a millionaire, isn't he?" I smiled.

"Yes," laughed James, "He wanted to see if you were any good. Now here's what he really wants to know...."

"All that glitters is not gold"

Long, blonde hair and an upturned chin addressed me. Her powder blue linen suit was finely tailored, and her skin was flawless. But Tina looked very uncomfortable. "Well, what can you tell me?" she asked.

As we moved into her face reading session, a very unusual thought was forming in my mind. "She looks beautiful, but there's something about her which is ugly." I mused that the word "ugly" is completely foreign to me even though I've seen all kinds of skin cancers and facial deformities. My heart was puzzled. I asked myself, "What is this about?" and the word "hooker" came up.

"Oh, that's it." I thought.

I never brought up her secret life. She stood up, gave me a hug and departed. The hairdressers nearby swarmed over to me to blurt out that the woman "worked" on 47th street. I just nodded.

Do You Have an Ear for Fashion?

Amidst the rustling of forks and napkins at the Interior Design Center of San Diego, I was reading the faces of some of the hundred guests. Halfway through, I became aware that 85% of them had the same shape ear – very long, thin, and narrow. I had never seen this feature before!

"Wow," I thought. "I wonder if people born with this ear shape will go into interior design as a career?" And over the years, it has proven to be so!

High School Memories

Fifty years old and gray at the temples a new student, Paul, raised his hand. "Barbara, can you tell me what I used to do in high school? I had a favorite thing I loved."

"Usually I like to look at the present or I get insights into the future, but let me see what comes up," I shut my eyes to focus. Going directly to my intuition I said, "The image I see is you sitting on the bench watching people wrestle."

As I opened my eyes, he was crying.

He breathed in, "I was never any good at wrestling, but it was my favorite sport. So I would go to every wrestling meet and watch them. I would sit on the bench and watch them wrestle."

Soul Patterns

Often, there is a feeling tone that comes from a client's energy – I call it a soul pattern or archetype of her personality. Some I've seen are the artist, healer, monk, lawmaker, businessman, and sorcerer. Two clients expressed this very clearly:

A man and his wife seated themselves for his session.

Midway through I mused, "The image of a lawmaker in the Old West keeps coming to me. I can see your husband with a rifle."

She laughed, "We call him the Sheriff. And he's also a gunsmith."

In another session, Margaret's eighteen year old red haired son nodded as I analyzed particulars of his thinking and emotional life.

"I keep getting the phrase 'White and Red Roses' as it relates to Russian history – some war. Do you know what that is?" I shrugged, confused.

"Yes, well, actually, that's the era in history that is my specialty in college. I speak fluent Russian, and I'm on my way to do an exchange program in the Soviet Union next month."

Before Dr. Sigmund Freud introduced psychiatry to western medicine, face reading (physiognomy) was the only system used throughout the world for understanding a person's character.

Face Reading - A Short-cut in Sales

"My name is Randy, and I live in North Carolina. My company sells computer circuits used in hospitals. I have a contract we're pitching to a man, Mark, who owns over a hundred hospitals. Can you tell me what to say to him?"

"What I need is a photo of you and a photo of him," I explained. "It's a matter of chemistry – you to him."

Randy brainstormed, "I'll start with getting to know him and his family. After all this is a million dollar contract. And he'll want to know about my background and our company. Then, I'll talk about the nursing shortage and how in the medical staff is getting more frustrated, and our product will help them with their stress so that they might give the patients better care...."

I stopped him. "This sounds great if you're talking to me. However, with Mark's face here's what he'll want. He's got a triangle-shaped face (across temples is large, apex is at the chin). That means he moves fast, thinks fast, and talks fast. You've got one minute to make your presentation. Start with money saved in the surgical areas by using your products, and then tell him about increased revenue to his hospital by adding another surgical case a day. End with money saved by decreasing in-house pharmacy bills with fewer meds needed by patients post-op. And as Mark has brown hair and brown eyes, I expect he'll have photos of his children on his desk. End with asking about his family and children."

Randy phoned me after the meeting. "We got the contract!" He was elated. "I did exactly what you said. Had I done what I wanted to do, we wouldn't have gotten it. Thanks, Barb!" And the contract lasted for years.

The Right Job (just in time!)

Lynne and I were walking on the beach near my house praying about which job she should take in medicine. Highly skilled and out of work, she was applying for jobs and networking like crazy. A son and a daughter in college and a house payment did not give the flexibility of a long holiday vacation. As we prayed I kept seeing the month "October" circled in my brain on a calendar.

"Your job is coming in October," I told her. "And you won't have to take a salary cut either."

"Well, Barb, it's mid-September already. How is this going to happen?" she looked at me incredulous.

Week after week we walked, prayed, and talked. Finally at the end of October things looked bleak. Then on October 31 the job offer came! She's now working for this incredible corporation at a salary above her last position, and they feel they are lucky to have her.

A Pregnancy, a New House, and Fruit Trees

"I'm six months pregnant, and we have to move. I'm getting pretty desperate, Barbara. It's almost Christmas!" Joan looked forlorn.

Quietly I prayed and got intuitively, "You're having twins – a boy and a girl?" (When I see it, the first part of an intuitive insight is usually a group of facts, so I ask the client if those are accurate. If they are, then the emotional or future intuitions that come with the facts also come true.)

"Why, yes! We just found out today on the ultrasound!" she blurted.

I continued, "I see the second week of February circled in my mind on a calendar. And a house with fruit trees and beige stucco front wall."

Well, I put this out of my mind till the phone call from Joan came in May.

"The twins want to meet you, and I want you to see our new house. We found it February 11 just as you said. We love it! We knew right away it was ours by the garden with peach trees and the beige stucco wall. Thank you!"

"The more unusual the features, the more accurate they are"

The live studio audience was assembled for my Learning Channel Show. A male volunteer came forward to have his face read. His ear was very unusual – the lower 1/3 was huge in size compared to the upper 2/3 (an earlobe found consistently in outdoor sportsmen.)

"You go camping and fishing every week-end?" I started.

"Yes! How did you know?" He was stunned.

How Emotional Healing Changed Two Children's Faces

My friend Elena opened her wallet and produced two color photos of the girls her family was about to adopt.

"In their birth family they had been severely traumatized, and I'm worried that we won't be able to help them." She looked apprehensive.

Two pixies, red haired toddlers, looked up at me from photos. I saw both had ears which extended at unusual angles – the upper ear rim turned down. (The ears reflect the neurological system, so unusual wavy edges or shapes may indicate the trauma was very deep. The emotions and spiritual life of a person are stepped down and recorded in the body and face, and I read the record of a person's life in their facial features. Having looked at FBI photos after 9-11 and studied past faces of criminals, WW II spies, gangsters, outlaws from the Old West, I had a basis of hundreds of photos of ears that indicated various degrees of trauma.) When part of the skin of upper ear flattens or turn down, clients have told me consistently that they do not remember large parts or years of their childhood.

Elena, her two sons and wonderful husband did adopt the girls and showered them with love and attention. Eight years later at a conference we were attending, Elena produced photos of her girls. I could see the beginning of radiance in their faces, and the ears were rotating back to normal positions alongside the head. As ears never change, this was a first to see!

Last summer when the family came to San Diego, we all went to the movies. I had the blessing of meeting her daughters in person. Their faces reflected emotional clarity. Their ear shapes were beautiful and completely normal.

Love and patience transformed their lives and their faces.

An Ear for Music

Ears that stick out reflect a person who can sensitively pick up sounds. That person usually has a gift for music. When the left ear is forward, the person will sing or play an instrument for fun or relaxation. If the right ear is forward, he may take his gift to a professional level. I was looking at a three-year-old child's photo noticing his left ear came forward. I suggested to his mom that she get him a drum set.

"I can't!" she replied in astonishment. "We already gave him one last year, and that's his favorite toy!"

Unlikely Benefactor

Surrounded by overhanging gardens and flowing fountains, I was ushered into the Persian-carpeted guest house. I could hear a woman just outside my door in a frenzy, talking to the kitchen chef about the inappropriate size of the croissants and their fillings. She spoke quickly in French, then Spanish. Pushing forward into the study to meet me, she extended her hand cordially.

I wondered, "What could I possibly say that would be useful to this woman who has everything?"

While she stretched out on the satin couch, I was drawn to her blue-grey eyes and her analytical, clear-thinking and unemotional gaze. A person with this color of blue-grey is fooled by no one and is impressed by only the finest in quality. This eye color is one I've seen only in people who have an interest in serving humanity privately or anonymously. I mumbled something to her about doing "selfless, humanitarian work," thinking that I was making a fool of myself because this seemed completely absurd!

Startled, she drew back and whispered, "Turn off the tape."

Then she leaned forward and said, "What I do all day is make and deliver meals for AIDS patients in this area. Only my husband knows that."

We smiled at each other and sat in silence.

Double Dipping

Craving a chocolate yogurt, I entered the near-by frozen yogurt shop. For several minutes I watched four women scurrying behind the counter helping the noon-hour customers. One of them seemed as though she didn't fit into the picture. It reminded me of childhood drawings of a line of ducks with only one wearing red goulashes.

Looking more closely at her face I asked, "Excuse me, are you a grade school teacher?" (She had very large cheeks with "teacher lines" - lines arching down the cheek on the right side of her face.) Then, she turned to the side, and I saw her down-turned nose, a facial feature reflecting financial planning.

I continued, "And you're the owner of this yogurt store, aren't you?

"Yes," she was astonished. "I am taking a six-month break from teaching third grade to start this business!"

What Your Teeth Reveal About Your Money Style

When a person's gums are visible on smiling, he will "swing with money" – budget then spend, budget then spend.

Fred and Maggie, a married couple, sat in my living room, both grinning broadly, revealing beautiful teeth with healthy pink gums showing widely above. He also had uneven eyebrow heights and visible front nostrils to his nose. These are all signs of someone who spends money frequently and is challenged by budgeting.

"So," Fred challenged, "I don't know if I buy this face reading stuff like Maggie does. What can you tell me about myself?"

"Well," I said, "You're not doing too well on your budget are you?"

The three of us broke out laughing.

Sex

A round ball on the chin with a dimple in it reveals a passionate life or a sensual nature. Sitting with me in my home, Elizabeth was producing one photo after another of her past boyfriends, asking me the nature of the relationships. Which of these men would be the most compatible for her, she wondered? She came to Larry and handed me the picture, smiling as she did so.

"So, what about this one, Barbara?"

Seeing the ball and dimple on the chin as the most pronounced part of his face, I asked, "Was this relationship 98% physical?"

She leaned forward. "100%," she laughed.

Just Horsing Around

Jamie, a woman with finely-textured blonde hair, blue eyes, a narrow jaw, and fine-pored skin sat before me. Her features all expressed sensitivity. With so many features for gentleness in her face, I wonder if she would find dealing with people too abrasive. Would she prefer the company of animals for companionship? If so, what animal would most appeal to her? Animals with gentleness, intelligence, and responsiveness? Might be horses.

I leaned forward. "Do you like horses?"

Astonished laughter and gasps broke out in the room.

Jamie replied, "I've loved horses since I was five. I own my own stable. Sometimes I have a hard time functioning in the world. I feel too sensitive for its hardness. Horses help me feel connected to life."

When Banking is Dangerous

Several years ago I was standing at the local bank depositing checks at the teller's station when I happened to turn around and look at the man behind me. The white (sclera) part in both of his eyes was showing below the iris (like Hitler's WW II men). Without hesitation I picked up my money and ran out of the bank. I turned just in time to see him put on a ski mask as he drew a gun to rob the bank.

How to Begin

Cultivate an Understanding Heart

Before Zen Masters teach meditation, there is a period of mental, inner preparation so as to enable the student to attune to the spirit of the discipline. Outer skills are imparted only after the inner framework has been laid. Because face reading reveals powerful and intimate information about people who would otherwise be total strangers to us, the following are some suggested Guidelines to help the beginner know "how" and "what" to say in response to the information we see in another's face.

It is important to prepare yourself first to be open and receptive. Before starting a session, I close my eyes and pray for the client, and ask that God guide what I say — that it be accurate, healing and useful.

Basic Principles

Seek to understand the person you are reading. Be compassionate.

The person must be able to integrate and understand what you say to them. The emotional information may be new for them. So leave them feeling positive and hopeful.

As a person heals from within and grows in wisdom, the face will reflect this new radiance. The face you are interpreting is like a computer printout of their emotional, spiritual and mental past. The physical transformation may not be obvious immediately as the soft tissue changes slower than the consciousness.

It is important to note that Face Reading as a tool for self-understanding is not a replacement for professional counseling or medical intervention. When particularly painful areas come up, I remind the client of the availability of individual, marital and family counseling, 12-step groups, prayer or church support, assertiveness training or other personal development classes.

Though accurate and insightful, face reading is not a psychic tool. Neither does it seek to give advice about what the client should or should not do.

How to Say What You See

Be gentle, kind and tactful.

Start with a positive attribute and emphasize the client's strengths (intelligence, sense of humor, determination). Gradually bring up one of their challenges or areas of stress as you see it in their facial features. Always phrase what you say with love. For example, "Are you working right now on issues of 'personal power'?" (positive) rather than, "I see that you are full of rage." (insulting)

Allow the client to draw you in. Let them share their feelings about what you see expressed in their face.

Frequently validate your intuitive perceptions by asking, "Is this true about you?" or by asking them to nod "yes" if you are accurate. If something you are saying is inaccurate, ask them to stop you. Their responding also lets you know that they understand and are integrating what is being said.

Always respect the client's sensitive emotional boundaries. Face reading is not: "I know all about you; you know nothing about me." Nor is it a subtle spiritual or emotional way to manipulate or overwhelm others.

Be alert for changes in the client's body language, which may indicate they are emotionally unable to take in what you are saying. Some visual cues may be a look of confusion, a sudden crossing of the arms or legs, or their physical move away from you. If you see these, stop! Ask the client to tell you what he or she is experiencing, and ask if he or she wants you to continue.

If you feel he *should* know something about him for his own good, but you feel he would be overwhelmed emotionally in the process, stop and look at your own motives for needing to tell him.

In a party setting, say only positive things to a person about their character as others may be listening.

> *Other factors that will affect our bodies, minds, attitudes, and thinking that are not included here: Neurological development, nutritional deficiencies, illnesses, our birth order with our siblings, childhood development, and family dynamics.*

FACIAL FEATURES
Drawings, Photos and Psychological Meanings

Hints for Quick Learning

The next section constitutes the bulk of the book. Each facial feature has a drawing, photo, and description of the psychological tendencies which will be accurate for someone with that feature. Also included is how that person will behave "on the job" and "on a date." Though there are thousands of features I have selected the most common ones, and the meanings in the boxes are universally accurate for people of all ethnic groups, ages, and genders.

The quickest way to learn face reading is to study one feature at a time. Spend a week looking at people's eyebrows – whether co-workers, family members, or photos from newspaper articles, and see if you find each meaning to be true for the person you are analyzing. Then go to eyes the next week. And so on.

When you do a composite character reading (looking at multiple features), choose the first five features that stand out on that person's face – those features which make him special. It might be red hair, high cheekbones, a square chin or flat eyebrows. Then look for themes in the character. If a psychological trait is strong in a person, it will show in multiples areas of his face. Conversely, if a tendency shows only once, it is not a major factor in the person's personality.

After reading this book you'll look at people in a completely different light. You will realize that every feature on their face tells a story of who they are, where they've been, and how they felt about it.

Hair Textures ~ Your Secret Sensitivity

Fine Hair

Psychological Meaning:

Sensitive, gentle, their nervous or digestive system can be upset under stress

On the Job:

"Do you think that co-worker likes me?" "My boss looked at me funny this morning. Do you think he's going to fire me?"

On a Date:

"Loud noise bothers me."

Thick Hair

Psychological Meaning:

Enjoys the outdoors, rugged, may be abrupt

On the Job:

"I need to walk at my lunch break. Could we have this meeting after my walk?" "I can work till 10 PM to finish this project tonight."

On a Date:

"Let's go hiking or to the park." "Could we go camping for the family vacation?"

Curly Hair

Psychological Meaning:

Lively, good sense of humor, playful

On the Job:

"To be happy I need to feel this job is fun!" "Tell me that story about the client."

On a Date:

"Play and joke with me. That will capture my heart. I love live comedy. 'Whose Line is it Anyway?' is my favorite TV show."

Straight Hair

Psychological Meaning:

Serious minded, straight forward, truthful

On the Job:

"If I give you my word, I'll be there. If I tell you 2 PM and I'm not there by 3 PM, start checking the hospitals!"

On a Date:

"You matter to me. I want to save up money so we can get married this year."

HAIR COLORS ~ DEGREE OF FLAIR AND DRAMA

Reminders: For someone who is Asian, African American, or Indian they will probably have black or brown hair, so you would ignore this facial feature (as it might be ethnically oriented) and move on to other features which show the person's uniqueness. Hair that is dyed will reflect a type #2 (how you like to look), so the meanings below will be relevant. If the person has gray hair, you might read the original color or ignore this feature.

Hair Color: Black

Psychological Meaning:

Dominant, intense, strong willed

On the Job:

"Don't get in my way." "I can handle extra responsibility on this project."

On a Date:

"Impress me. Show me what you've got. Why should I be interested in you? Tell me."

Hair Color: Brown

Psychological Meaning:

Family oriented, looks for emotional warmth and sincerity in others

On the Job:

"I work to put my kids through school. I have their photos every-where in my office."

On a Date:

"Before we get more serious, I need you to meet my daughter and son. (Let's see if they like you.)"

Hair Color: Blond

Psychological Meaning:

Sunny disposition, fun loving, self-confident

On the Job:

"Let me lighten your day with donuts." "What can we do with this angry client to win back his business with our firm?"

On a Date:

"Mountain biking sounds like fun, but can we still stay in the B + B with the spa massages?" "Can we focus more on the positive in our relationship?"

Hair Color: Red

Psychological Meaning:

Fiery, intense, dramatic

On the Job:

"Make me the project manager. I can do it." "I don't want it to be . . .! It needs to be like this or I'll quit."

On a Date:

"How are you in bed?" "I'm very passionate and need someone who is a good lover."

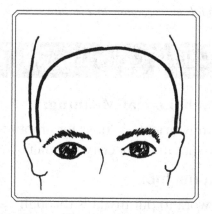

Forehead: Round

Psychological Meaning:

People person, has many long term friendships, good in relationships

On the Job:

"Let me plan the company picnic." "I'd love to take this new client out for dinner and then show them the town." "We should check on (client) Jane today and see how she is doing."

On a Date:

"Let's double date tonight." "I want to have dinner with the whole family – yes, all my 10 brothers."

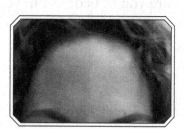

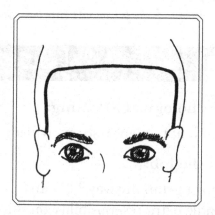

Forehead: Square

Psychological Meaning:

Career driven, works long hours at the office, focused

On the Job:

"Sorry, sweetie, I can't talk on the phone right now. I'm preparing the draft for . . . I'll phone you at midnight on my break."

On a Date:

"I don't have time for a personal life. Can't see you."

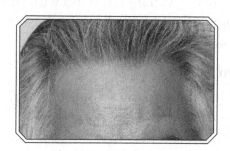

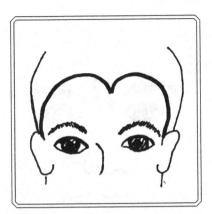

Forehead: Widow's Peak

Psychological Meaning:

Likes relaxed life style, dresses casually often in blue jeans and sweats, creative, doesn't like to be told what to do

On the Job:

"Give me the specs (facts), and I'll put all the art work together for you by tomorrow morning."

On a Date:

"Let's explore together what we want to do for our future." "Let's go to the theater tonight."

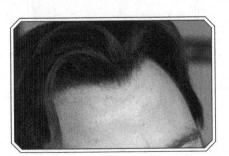

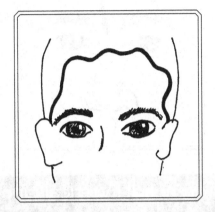

Forehead: Uneven Hairline

Psychological Meaning:

Childhood may have been chaotic (many siblings) or non-nurturing

On the Job:

"I have trouble with my boss when she reminds me of my dominant, critical mother."

On a Date:

"Help me feel secure and let me know I'm special to you."

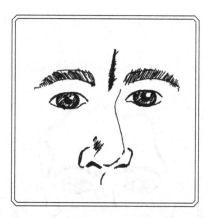

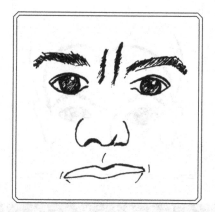

Forehead: 1 Vertical Line (above the nose)

Psychological Meaning:

Goes in a different direction than family of origin (geographically, financially, emotionally and/or spiritually)

On the Job:

"I pioneered this invention 10 years before anyone else. I like to work independently."

On a Date:

"Can you be independent also? (or at least admire me for being so)?"

Forehead: 2 Vertical Lines (above the nose)

Psychological Meaning:

Good concentration, focus, worry or compulsive with details

On the Job:

"I've been doing this Project for five hours and forgot to eat today."

On a Date:

"Did I turn off the stove before we left on vacation? Let me check it (for the fourth time.)"

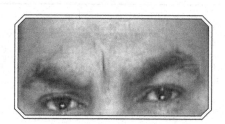

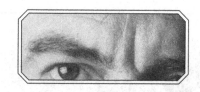

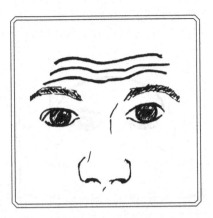

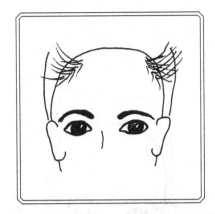

Forehead: 3 Horizontal Lines (across wide area above eyes)

Psychological Meaning:

Wealth and good fortune, financial success, logical thinker

On the Job:

"Where should I put my new investments?"

On a Date:

"Show me that you have confidence, and I'll be attracted to you."
"I'll pay for that."

Forehead: Wispy Corners (tiny wisps of hair in the outer corners of the corners/forehead)

Psychological Meaning:

Her mother had a significant impact in his life (positive or negative)

On the Job:

"I love my female boss. I learn so much from her. She's my mentor."

or

"My boss is critical and demanding, and I have a hard time setting good boundaries with her. This happened with my Mom, and I just freeze around my boss."

On the Date:

"If you want to marry me, you'd better love my mom. She comes over often, and we talk on the phone all the time."

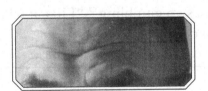

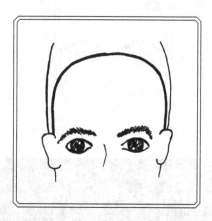

Forehead: High
(related to distance from eyes)

Psychological Meaning:

Clear thinker, planner, strategist, and thinks in big terms

On the Job:

"Let me develop the five-year plan." "I'm concerned with global warming." "What do you think?"

On a Date:

"I need a partner I can talk to about my ideas and plans."

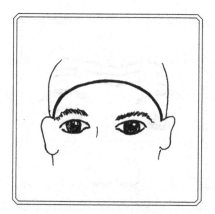

Forehead: Low (short)
(related to distance from eyes)

Psychological Meaning:

Impulsive, street smart, trusts his "gut" instincts with people

On the Job:

"I just met Jerry and I liked him, so I loaned him my car keys to drive to Mexico. He took the company car and sold it in Mexico. Sorry." "As a psychologist I don't always listen to the words my client is saying. I feel it in my gut if he is lying."

On a Date:

"Let's go gambling." "I like it when you drive fast."

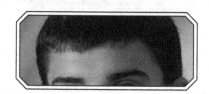

How Your See the World
Eye Colors, Sizes, and Shapes

Eye Color: Blue

Psychological Meaning:

Is thinking 24/7, never has enough book shelves for his books

Light blue: peaceful, low physical endurance, may be passive

Deep Blue: left brained, emotionally analytical, traditional religious values or beliefs

On the Job:

"Let's develop our Team's goals and philosophy, our Mission statement."

On a Date:

"What do you think about that?" "I love spending time in book stores."

Eye Color: Brown

Psychological Meaning:

Family oriented, affectionate, friends and family are very important, warm hearted

On the Job:

"If you project personal warmth and sincerity, then I'll do business with you."

On a Date:

"Let's cuddle by the fireplace and watch a family movie." "I love romantic comedies." "How many children do you want?"

Eye Color: Blue-Gray

Psychological Meaning:

Likes to analyze the emotions of a situation: "He said", "I said," "I should have said", is often a humanitarian and benefit focused

On the Job:

"If he says . . . , then I'll do . . . , and then I expect she'll say . . ."

On a Date:

"What do you mean I'm analyzing you too much?"

Eye Color: Green

Psychological Meaning:
Curious, always learning and taking classes

On the Job:
"Does this company pay for continuing education?" "I want to go for my Master's degree."

On a Date:
"What did you learn today?" "What are you thinking about right now?" "Do you enjoy literature?" "I love the Discovery Channel." "Let's take a class together."

Eye Color: Hazel

Psychological Meaning:
Multitasks at all times (does 20 projects), easily bored, needs variety, mentally agile. Interested in topics of healing and insight

On the Job:
"The reason I love being a doctor is that every patient's situation is different, and it lets me be creative in helping each one." "I'd love to travel on the job." "How many ways can we do this advertising?"

On a Date:
"Let's take classes together." "What can we do this weekend that we haven't done before?"

Eye Color: Gray

Psychological Meaning:
Emotionally cool, detached, analytical, private, can be secretive

On the Job:
"I work for the FBI." "I don't want to share the information I've gathered on this case with you."

On a Date:
"I need a partner who doesn't need a lot of emotional support from me." "I need some quiet time."

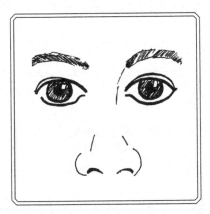

Eyes: Large Size

Psychological Meaning:

Sentimental, soft hearted, generous, others may take advantage of him

On the Job:

"I was walking the older woman's dog, and I stopped to see her photos of her kids. She wants to be our client now." "Tell me your feelings about your investments so I'll know how to help you with them."

On a Date:

"What do you feel about....?" "I love red roses, words of affection, and romantic songs." "I'll keep the book of the poems you wrote me forever."

Eyes: Small

Psychological Meaning:

Picks up minute details in other's behavior or in environment

On the Job:

"Has Jenny been 10 minutes late every day this week?"

On a Date:

"Last Christmas at the party I noticed you liked the pink roses at the restaurant so I got you a bouquet of 12 today."

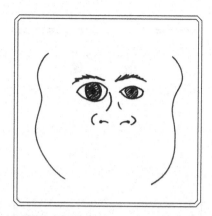

Eyes: Right Eye is Bigger

Psychological Meaning:

Career is the focus for first ½ of life. Once settled, he looks at his emotional needs and feelings.

On the Job:

"I'm here 15 hours a day. And I can work 7 days a week." (Age 20) "Let's have yoga classes for employees to decrease their stress so they can be more effective at work." (Age 60)

On a Date:

"Are you involved in your work also?" "Right now it's important that I establish myself in a career and save for a family." (Age 20) Later, "I've been very successful in my early years, and now I want to spend time playing with my grandchildren." (Age 60)

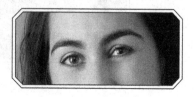

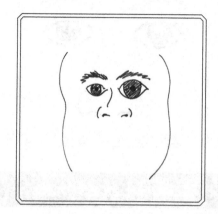

Eyes: Left Eye is Bigger

Psychological Meaning:

The first ½ of his life he focuses on who he is and his emotional healing. After 35, he focuses on his career.

On the Job:

"I started this career at age 36, and I love it. It's what makes me really happy. I've finally found my niche."

On a Date:

"I'm a bit of a later bloomer. Can you wait for me?"

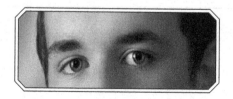

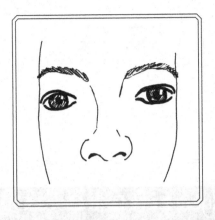

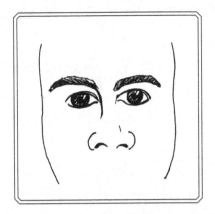

Eyes: Wide Set

(distance between the two eyes is wider than the length of one eye)

Psychological Meaning:

Kind hearted, sees big picture, humanitarian, may shows up late for appointments.

On the Job:

"I need to feel that this company project not only makes money, but that it serves a greater good."

On a Date:

"I want to go to be in the Peace Corps in Africa. Will you wait for me to come back?" "What are your values?" "Do you think of others?"

Eyes: Close Set

(distance between the two eyes is less than the length of one eye)

Psychological Meaning:

Detail oriented, precision driven, perfectionist, enjoys research

On the Job:

"Did you get my 15th draft of the bird bath? Did you notice the fifth beam to the left has changed by ½ inch?"

On a Date:

"I want the music, ambience, flowers to be just right for you."

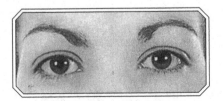

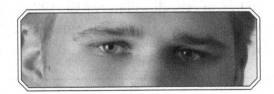

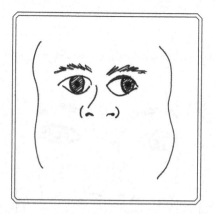

Eyes: Left Eye Goes Out

(left eye goes away from the center/midline when he is looking straight ahead. Psychological meaning is accurate only if this facial feature is not strabismus – a childhood anatomical condition where the eye muscles are not balanced.)

Eyes: Deep Set

(in profile, the eyes are in-set)

Psychological Meaning:
Deep thinker, philosophical, introspective

On the Job:
"What are our long term goals with client Mr. J?" "Is what we are currently offering in our advertising for our highest good?" "How can we offer better HR packages for our employees to help them take care of their children's health?"

On a Date:
"I'm looking for a partner who cares about serving other people." "Do you ever do volunteer work?" "Which spiritual path interests you the most?"

Psychological Meaning:
May sabotage a smoothly running life by creating dramatic and sudden turmoil

On the Job:
"I was making $2000 an hour doing modeling, but I got into cocaine and lost my job."

On a Date:
"I want to marry you, but also want to sleep with your best friend."

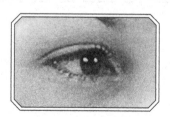

Action Oriented or Planner Eyelids

Eyes: Visible Eyelids

Psychological Meaning:

Action-oriented, doer, likes to get things done right away

On the Job:

"We can set this up right now. Why wait?" "Give the project to me. I'll do it right now."

On a Date:

"Let's go clean out the garage. We can figure who we want to give the things to as we work. We'll just start on it now before we lose momentum."

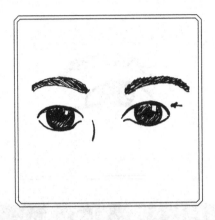

Eyes: Non-Visible Eyelids

Psychological Meaning:

Planner, sets up systems for other people to follow, list maker

On the Job:

"Let me develop a delivery dispatch system so it'll make it easier for our people out in the field."

On a Date:

"I'm making lists of animals we want to see at the Wild Animal Park so we won't waste any time."

TRUST ISSUES IN THE LOWER EYE AREA

Eye Area: Flat Lower

(below the eye)

Psychological Meaning:

Cautious, wary, "waits to see"

On the Job:

"I like the new boss, but 'I'm from Missouri.' Let him show me if he'll be good for our company's employees and our financial profits."

On a Date:

"I go slowly getting to know you. I might have some trust issues, but please give us time to see if we're good."

Eye Area: Rounded Lower

Psychological Meaning:

Romantic, sentimental, loves to keep mementos of good times

On the Job:

"I still have the first honorary promotion pin the company gave me 20 years ago."

On a Date:

"I'll keep this flower he gave me on our first date forever in my scrapbook. I love pink roses, candles, soft music, fire places, walks on the beach at sunset." "Will you remember our Anniversary?"

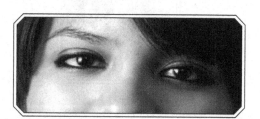

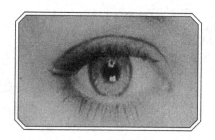

Eye Area: "Teacher Lines"

(lines fan downward across the cheek area)

Psychological Meaning:

Gifted teacher, writer, speaker, correct grammar is important, a good story teller

On the Job:

"I'd love to explain how to use our new product to this client."

On a Date:

"Talk to me. Tell me all about you." "Can you teach me how to change the oil in my car?" "If you say 'ain't' I'll notice it." "I hope you enjoy my sense of humor. I love it when you verbally play with me."

Eye Area: Bags Under

Psychological Meaning:

Unresolved emotional grieving

On the Job:

"I could never please my dad, and it was frustrating. My male boss is like that also." (if unresolved)

On a Date:

"I need to share my emotional pain with you on this subject. Will you listen to me and be patient?"

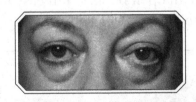

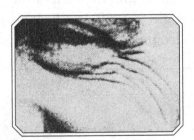

EYEBROWS
Degree of Friendliness

Eyebrows: Low Set

(related to distance between the eyes and the eyebrows)

Psychological Meaning:

Friendly, easily approachable, could be over familiar

On the Job:

"I'm very popular at work. I'm the center of what's happening. People tell me everything."

On a Date:

"I'm an open book." "I'm easy to get to know."

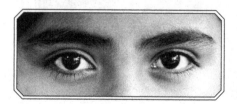

Eyebrows: High Set

(related to distance between the eyes and the eyebrows)

Psychological Meaning:

High standards, not easily impressed by other people, very loyal to their friends, selective of close friends

On the Job:

"I have 50 acquaintances, but only 3 people I can depend on."

On a Date:

"Take me to the symphony." "I love quality, and my idea of the perfect gift is a gift certificate from Nordstroms."

Eyebrows: Thick or Bushy

Psychological Meaning:

Abrupt, dominant, intense

On the Job:

"I want it NOW!" "I love it! I'm excited about your idea for the company!"

On a Date:

"I know you want to do . . . but I am the head of the house here." "I love shows like 'Boston Legal' and 'The Apprentice.' I don't want to watch a comedy."

Thin Eyebrows

Psychological Meaning:

Very sensitive, gentle nature, may be high strung under pressure

On the Job:

"At 3:30-5:00 PM I have a blood sugar drop and head for the chocolate, coffee machine, or sugar."

On a Date:

"I'm gentle and kind." "Let me know your feelings and thoughts so I can understand you better."

Eyebrows: Arched

Psychological Meaning:

Powerful, dramatic, artistic, loves plays, dance, theater. Enjoys vibrant colors. May have a short temper.

On the Job:

"I love stirring things up at work." "Let me mentor the new employees."

On a Date:

"Let's go to the symphony tonight…or the opera." "I'd like to redecorate your house – reds and oranges would give it life."

Eyebrows: Rounded

Psychological Meaning:

Creates harmonious relationships, likes a peaceful home environment.

On the Job:

"I really want our team to get along. Let's work this out so everyone is happy here."

On a Date:

"Could you not play that drum set? I really need quiet to recharge." "I'm a homebody." "Feng shui would be interesting."

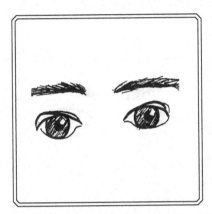

Eyebrows: Flat, Straight

Psychological Meaning:

A projects person, shy, introverted

On the Job:

"In the interview I might have a hard time selling myself." "My work will speak for me." "I love to work independently."

On a Date:

"I'm a bit shy. Be patient with getting to know me." "Want to play video games? I know them all."

Eyebrows: Unibrow

(one unbroken eyebrow)

Psychological Meaning:

Intense or aggressive

On the Job:

"I will not compromise!" "I don't care that people are losing their jobs. I've got mine."

On a Date:

"I don't like animals. Why do you have them?" "I'm moving ahead with this whether you like it or not."

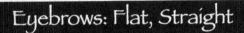

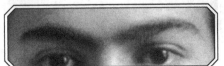

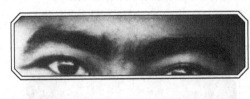

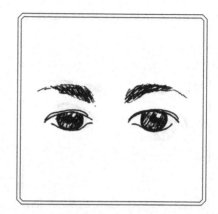

Eyebrows: Uneven Heights

*(one lower, one higher –
doesn't matter which one)*

Psychological Meaning:

Money goes up and down (The worst finances are from ages 20-29). Money gets better as person becomes older.

On the Job:

"I'm hesitant to invest in your new venture. I've lost so much money early in my life." (Age 35)

On a Date:

"Are you paying for this date?"
"Are you financially stable?"

Eyebrows: Half is Strong, Outer Half is Pale/Thin

Psychological Meaning:

Struggled emotionally in the first half of life. The second half is easier.

On the Job:

(Age 24) "I give 150%."

On a Date:

"I need tenderness and patience to establish trust and intimacy with you."

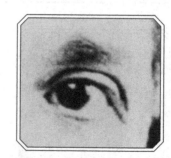

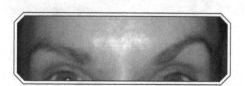

CHEEKS
Degree of Your Personal Warmth and Feeling

Cheeks: High Cheek Bones

Psychological Meaning:

Loves to travel, needs to be self-employed, high spirited

On the Job:

"I'd rather do my independent project right now than join you at the company's social event." "I love going to Brazil. My passport is always up to date."

On a Date:

"I go to the beat of my own drum. Want to follow me?" "Want to go on an adventure with me?"

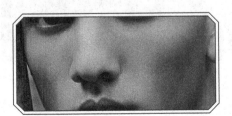

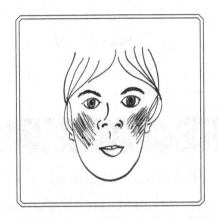

Cheeks: Flat

Psychological Meaning:

Intellectualizes his feelings, cool emotionally, lack of mother's nurturing as a child

On the Job:

"What do you mean I don't share my work?" "I didn't notice that I had hurt the client's feelings"

On a Date:

"I don't know what I feel about you at all. Should I know?"

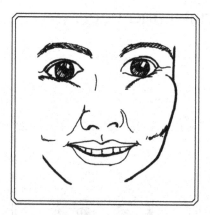

Cheeks: Rounded

Psychological Meaning:

Feelings oriented, sensitive, loving, big hearted. They make issues personal.

On the Job:

"Let's help our client, Mary, feel she can come to us with any problems she has with the new product." "I need to know that I am personally making a difference with my work."

On a Date:

"How are you feeling?" "Listen to my feelings (a way to make me feel special.)" "I love flowers, words of affection, and soft touches."

Dimples on Cheeks

Psychological Meaning:

Fun loving, great sense of humor, sees joy in everything

On the Job:

"This database is so tedious. What can we do to have fun while creating it?" This person is the best company hostess to entertain new clients from out of town. They'll love her!

On a Date:

"Do you know how to have fun?"

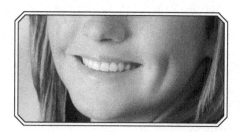

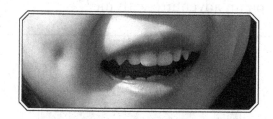

NOSE
Your Financial Potential

Nose: Large

Psychological Meaning:

Wealth, spiritual or financial abundance

On the Job:

"How can I invest this new wealth to make more?"

On a Date:

"I'll pay!" "I like being generous with those who are less fortunate." "Let me buy this for you." (The ideal money nose!)

Nose: Hawk

(large, long nose that points down at an angle)

Psychological Meaning:

Puts his nose in other's business, under pressure - treacherous

On the Job:

"Tell me your juicy gossip. I might use it against you." "What did you say about John, Mary, and Teri?"

On a Date:

"Don't trust me. I'm not always safe." (unless the rest of my facial features are wonderful.)

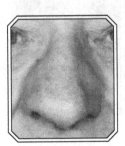

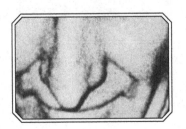

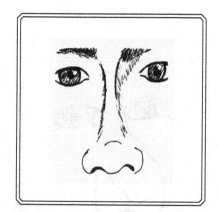

Nose: Nostrils Visible

(must be on eye level with client)

Psychological Meaning:

"Money comes in; money goes out." They spend as they have it!

On the Job:

"I just spent $6,000 for a chair for the boss. Was that too much?"

On a Date:

To the partner: "You better handle our budget and money." "We have a little extra money this month. How about a week at the spa?"

Nose: Narrow Bridge

Psychological Meaning:

Enjoys classical string instruments, perfectionist, loner

On the Job:

"This is the 20th revision of the bird bath. Do you think I'm over invested in this project?"

On a Date:

"You forgot to put the orange lid on the orange pan." "I love violin music." "I need some space."

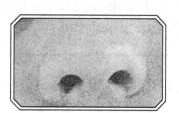

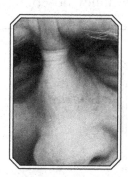

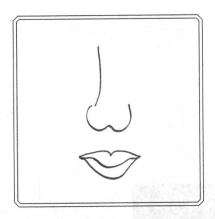

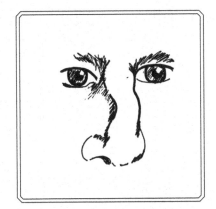

Nose: Split Tip

Psychological Meaning:

In his/her first romantic relationship with the opposite sex he had his heart broken.

On a Job: --------

On a Date:

"If you remind me of my first love, I'm going to run for the hills." If young: "I might have some trust issues in a romantic relationship. Be patient with me, and I can work them out."

Nose: Breaks Along It

(deviation of the septum or where the nose angles to the right or to the left)

Psychological Meaning:

Traumas or major life changes – career moves, divorce, challenges with children, geographical moves, illness, death of loved one. The years for the trauma are measured from the nose bridge down:
• Nose bridge: during teens
• 1/3 down: mid to late 20s
• 1/2 down: in 30s

On the Job:

"I just started a new business after my divorce and illness."

On a Date:

(after) "I'm stable again!" "Will you be patient with me as I start over?"

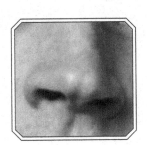

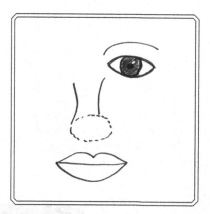

Nose: Ball on the Tip

Psychological Meaning:

Center of news, information and gossip, loves doing research and gathering information

On the Job:

"Let me do the internet search on that." "I can put together all the projects and inventions that have been done on this topic for you."

On a Date:

"People tell me everything." "I know inner gossip of everyone in my group." "I'm the life of the party."

LIPS
Romance and Intimacy Quotient

Mouth: Large (Wide)

Psychological Meaning:

Generous, affectionate, warm

On the Job:

"How can I make your job easier for you?" "Here, let me do this for you." (pat on the back)

On a Date:

"I would love to rub your back. Here, lie down next to me." "I love bathing the baby – it's so much fun." "Give me a hug."

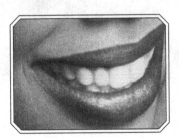

Mouth: Small

(size of nose or slightly bigger)

Psychological Meaning:

Self-absorbed, rich fantasy life, makes great actor, can be dangerous

On the Job:

"My needs are the only ones that matter in this company." "I am an artist and love to create."

On a Date:

"I need you to fuss over me." "I want your complete devotion." "What do you mean I'm narcissistic?" "Do your needs exist?"

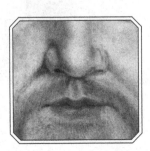

Mouth: Lines Down at Mouth Corners

Psychological Meaning:

Sadness, depression, emotional losses

On the Job:

"We lost another contract. I feel very depressed by this."

On a Date:

"My glass is ½ empty." "I'm a realist." "I'm still recovering from my divorce. Listen to my feelings to get close to me."

Mouth: Lower Lip Bigger

Psychological Meaning:

Takes in information and doesn't gossip, good with confidences, sensual

On the Job:

"You can tell me anything about your finances. I'll never repeat it to anyone."

On a Date:

"You can share your feelings with me. I'm safe to talk to."

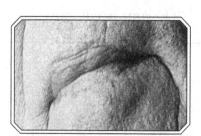

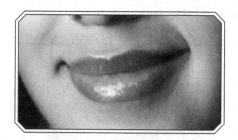

Mouth: Thin Lips

Psychological Meaning:

Terse, business like, focuses on facts, objective

On the Job:

"Don't ask me about my daughter's surgery while we are at work. It's not professional." "Let's be objective on this budget and see how we can cut back."

On a Date:

"I don't know how to express emotional warmth to you. So let me rotate your tires."

Mouth: Larger Upper Lip

Psychological Meaning:

Giver, loves to take care of others, may want to see how his gift is being used, at times gives too much

On the Job:

"We gave this contribution to the United Way. Can you get me the receipts and cost analysis of how they spent it?"

On a Date:

"Here, let me buy that car for you. Are you going to be driving it only to work?"

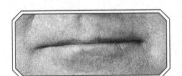

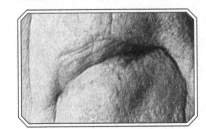

Teeth: Space Between 2 Front Teeth

Psychological Meaning:

Between the ages of 3-6 his father was away (working, army, divorce)

On the Job:

"I really appreciate my older (man) boss who is my mentor. He helps me know how to move forward with the company's vision."

On a Date:

"I might be a bit nervous about meeting your dad on our first date."

Teeth: Chaotic

Psychological Meaning:

Possible lack of inner nurturing as a child, chaotic family of origin

On a Job:

"I might have a hard time focusing in a career as a family divorce lawyer because I would get too absorbed in the emotions of the injured children."

On a Date:

"My family wasn't so close, so I really want to put energy into this relationship to make it work."

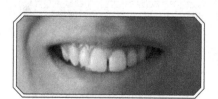

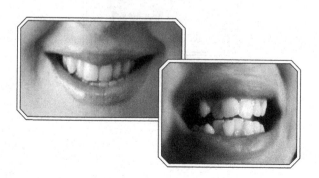

Large Front Teeth

Psychological Meaning:

Strong willed, stubborn, fixed

On the Job:

"I intend to set my goal for sales: 500 units this month. Next month I'll be at 600, even if I have to work 10 hours per day."

On a Date:

"I've considered your point of view, but I want to do it my way." "I can be strong willed, but I can also be fair."

Small Teeth

Psychological Meaning:

Quick learner, auditory and visual learner

On the Job:

"Show me how to do this, and I can make another one quickly."

On a Date:

"If you'll show me how you like your neck rubbed, I'd be happy to do this to get rid of your headache."

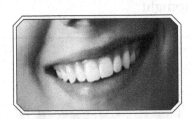

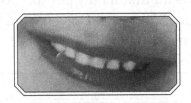

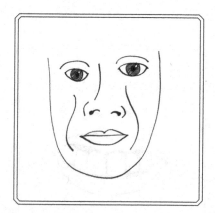

Visible Gum Line

Psychological Meaning:

"I budget, and then I spend." "I swing with money – I save and then I make big purchase."

On the Job:

"I might not be the best choice as accountant for the company."

On a Date:

"Last week I bought a sports car. Had been saving up by taking my lunch for about a year. What do you mean that'll only pay for gas?". "I have $50 saved. Do you want to help me spend it?"

Naso-Labial Lines

(Go in a circle around the mouth and outer nose)

Psychological Meaning:

Able to talk with anyone about anything. Very outgoing and great communication skills.

On the Job:

"Let me take that new client to lunch and explain the project to his company." "How are you today?"

On a Date:

"I can make you feel right at ease." "Tell me about your children." "Want to go to a stand-up comedy club tonight?"

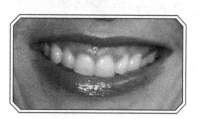

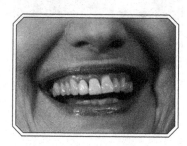

EAR HEIGHTS
Markings and Lobes

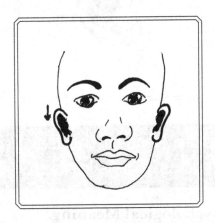

Ears: High Placed	Ears: Low Placed

(related to an imaginary horizontal line drawn through the mid-point of the eyes)

Psychological Meaning:

Academically brilliant, has two college degrees or a good memory

On the Job:

"I graduated first in my MIT class in engineering, and I want to go back for a MBA."

On a Date:

"What's in your mind that can keep my interest?" "What did you think about that play?"

(related to an imaginary horizontal line drawn through the mid-point of the eyes)

Psychological Meaning:

Late bloomer, comes into his own between ages 35-50

On the Job:

"I became the owner of this company at age 36. I had worked at jobs that built up to this one. Now I'm a huge success – finally!"

On a Date:

"I have great plans and dreams. Will you listen to mine? What are yours?"

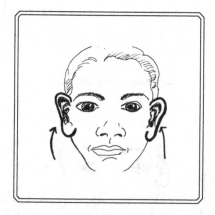

Middle Area of the Ear Protrudes, Turns Inside Out

Psychological Meaning:

Interest in alternative medicine, yoga, Pilates, mediation, chiropractic, acupuncture, energy work, feng shui, or creative ideas

On the Job:

"You have a headache? There's a place on the pad of the thumb that can relieve that if you massage it." "I would much rather work in an herb store than a hospital."

On a Date:

"Can you meet me at the Hatha class at 8:00 AM?" "I'd much rather go on a spiritual retreat than go water skiing." "Have you tried garlic for reducing your cholesterol?"

Ears: Long Lobes

Psychological Meaning:

Spiritual seeker, wants to understand Truth, interested in Inner transformation. In artistic renderings of Buddha, he has ear lobes almost touching his shoulders.

On the Job:

"Does our company have a humanitarian mission statement?" "Is that project ethical?"

On a Date:

"Let's go to the meditation retreat this summer." "Do you want to do the yoga Class with me?"

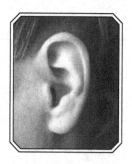

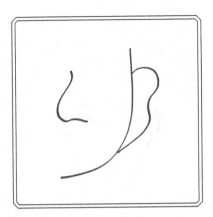

No Ear Lobe

(ear comes straight out from the head)

Psychological Meaning:

Knows immediately if he likes you or not, makes snap judgments (Often they are right!)

On the Job:

"I don't think that person will last as the boss' secretary." "I don't feel I can trust that manager with this information."

On a Date:

"There's no chemistry here. I'm going to go." "There is chemistry here. I'll stay for dinner."

Ears of Unusual Shape

(ears rotate out from head with unusual edges and shapes)

Psychological Meaning:

Neurological challenges, possible erratic behavior or learning disabilities

On the Job:

"I don't understand what you wanted on that project."

On a Date:

Be careful to watch his/her behavior over time and not his/her words of endearment to you. "I enjoy action war movies. Violence doesn't bother me."

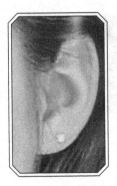

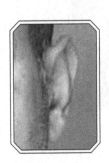

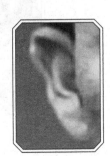

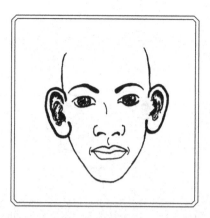

Large Ears

(proportional to total size of the head)

Psychological Meaning:

Tunes into the big picture, good listener, people tell them everything, jobs in communications match them well

On the Job:

"I love being a psychologist because I enjoy listening to people." "People tell me everything."

On a Date:

"I love symphonies." "Talk to me. Tell me all about you and your family."

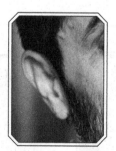

Small Ears

Psychological Meaning:

He hears "qpf" when someone says "abc," difficult communication skills, may be self-absorbed or devious

On the Job:

"I have my own plans for this project."

On a Date:

"I thought what you wanted was this. I misunderstood you." "I need you to write down or repeat back to me things that you said so we can make sure we understood each other."

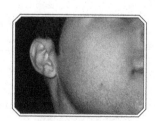

CHIN UP!

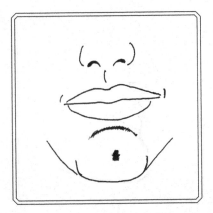

Chin: Center Dimple

Psychological Meaning:

Passionate, loves people who live their dreams, has high level of physical energy, sensual.

On the Job:

"I'll lead the mountain climbing trail." "I love to listen to the stories of people who do something out of the norm."

On a Date:

"Do you love life?" "I'm intense about how I live life. Are you?"

Rounded Chin

Psychological Meaning:

Loves animals and children

On the Job:

"I love being a dolphin trainer at Sea World." "I'm the owner of this pre-school, and it's my life work. I love it." "I want to be an elementary school teacher." "Let me plan the games for the children at the company picnic." "I love working as a vet."

On a Date:

(Hopefully not the first date!) "When we get married, do you want to have children?" "I have six dogs. Do you like animals?"

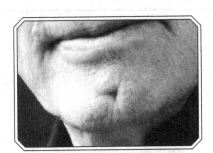

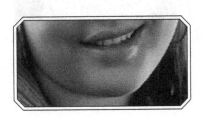

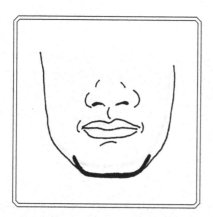

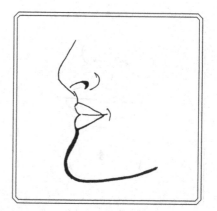

Square Chin

Psychological Meaning:

Able to draw wealth, financially dynamic

On the Job:

"I developed a new way to make paint which has never been done before, and that made me a millionaire."

On a Date:

"I will provide for you." "Let me work hard, so I can save for our future financially."

Chin Projects Forward

Psychological Meaning:

Dynamic, moves ahead with his goals, makes lemonade out of lemons, eats problems for breakfast

On the Job:

"What do we need at this company? Show me where and how, and I'll do it."

On a Date:

"I like a partner to appreciate my go-getting spirit." "I will work for you and the children." "Let's go do active projects together."

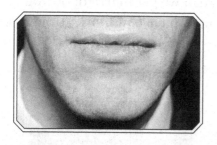

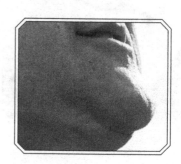

JAWS
How You Move Forward in the World

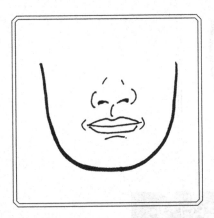

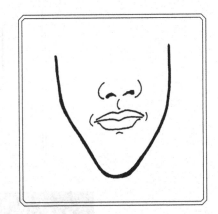

Jaw: Broad

Psychological Meaning:

Strong will power, dynamic, impatient if he perceives others to be lazy or irresponsible, can be rigid or abusive if other features are not good

On the Job:

(Good) "I am taking command of this team." "You can rely on me." (With poor features) "I quit. I'm going to go drink beer and ride my motorcycle."

On a Date:

(Good) "Let me carry you." "I am very responsible, and can take care of you and the kids." (With poor features) "I hit things when I'm mad."

Jaw: Narrow

Psychological Meaning:

Kind, gentle, shy, needs good emotional boundaries, may have a hard time marketing his talents if self-employed

On the Jobs:

"I'd rather be in the art room creating the film than presenting it to the group in the studio."

On a Date:

"I'm gifted but shy." "I have a lot to offer so don't overlook me for someone more outwardly assertive."

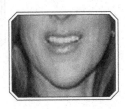

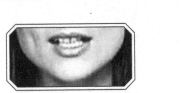

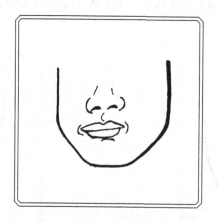

Jaw: Left Side Bigger

Psychological Meaning:

Self-critical, harder on himself than he is on others

On the Job:

"I should have done that (perfectly) from the start."

On a Date:

"I should have gotten you the white baby's breath with the yellow bud roses." "I feel horrible that I did…. (not a big thing). Everyone noticed."

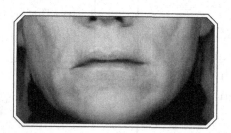

MOLES

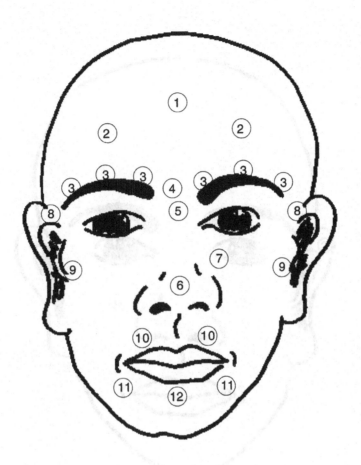

1. Matures at an early age

2. Would be a good wife/husband

3. Well off $

4. Change professions frequently

5. $ losses or problems with opposite sex

6. Be careful of financial losses

7. May travel in foreign lands late in life

8. More gifted than normal

9. (mid-ear) Person is ambitious

10. In men: major transformation. In women: may have OB/GYN problems

11. Quick to make decisions

12. Serious thinker at young age

MOLES

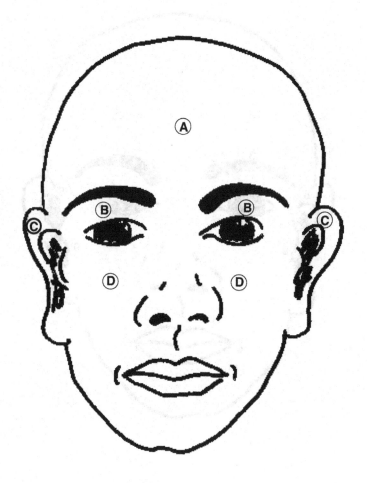

A. Forehead Moles: Career-driven and intense

B. Eye-area Moles: Fickle or intimacy avoiding

C. Ear Moles: Good position in life. Person feels emotionally supported, good fortune

D. High Cheek Moles: Power and strength, likely to be in a position of influence

FACIAL SHAPES

 SQUARE:

strong leader, Rock of Gibraltor for others,
solid, may feel lonely in management role

 DIAMOND:

survivor, emotionally tough and self-reliant,
loves to travel, wants to be self employed

 RECTANGLE:

scholarly, sensitive, intelligent, fearful in new
situations

 TRIANGLE:

writer, personality is fire-like, quick thinker,
drives fast, impatient, visionary, radical
opinions

 CIRCLE:

loves food and good cook, makes great sales
person, easy going

OVAL:

nurturing, friendly, peace maker

FACIAL FEATURE REVIEW
(Write underneath one meaning for each)

Hair Colors:

Black

Blonde

Brown

Red

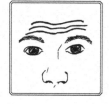 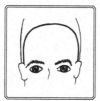 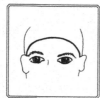

Eye Colors:

Blue

Blue-Gray

Brown

Gray

Green

Hazel

  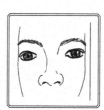 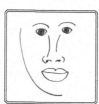 

 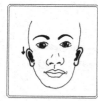 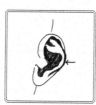  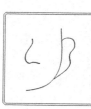 

  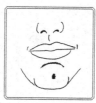   

FACIAL FEATURES AND YOU

If your goal is self-realization or eliminating root causes of personal suffering, then face reading is an invaluable tool for introspection. It is personal, intimate, and accurate as it mirrors the link between your body and mind. It is a clear and unbiased starting point for self knowledge.

Easy Exercise for Introspection

- Look at your face in a mirror.

- What are the first five facial features you see?

- What do they mean psychologically? (Look them up in the book.)

- Are there any themes in these psychological meanings?

- If so, what are some psychological opposites?

For example, if your features reveal you to be spiritual, gentle, sensitive, musical, and soft-spoken, a person whose character is opposite to yours might be assertive, aggressive, direct, overbearing, loud or out-spoken. You might say, "Well, I don't want to be that way!" which would make sense. However, do you have repeated stress or conflicts around individuals who express your opposites? If so, then these opposite tendencies become for you areas of your "life lessons." Everyone's life lessons are individual. The goal in the example above is not to become aggressive or overbearing, but to be able to use some of our opposite traits when we need them in a given situation. It would be like taking them from a tool box called "All Behaviors." When we need to be assertive or direct or to defend a position, we can pull up those qualities. A great saint, Sri Yukteswar, spoke of being emotionally "freely expressive" with the quality of love being uppermost.

Facial Features Which Reflect "TOO MUCH" or "too little"

- Aggression ("too much" self) vs. Timidity ("too little" self): Aggressive facial features (Chapter on "Dangerous Facial Features") include white sclera under the irises of the eyes, a strong, huge jaw that juts forward, or a short forehead. Timidity or excessive shyness can be seen in a receding chin, a very narrow face, or one front tooth blocking the other front tooth.

- Narcissism ("too much" self) vs. Lack of Confidence ("too little" self). Narcissism can show in features as a tiny mouth, small ears, vacant eye tone, or flat cheeks. Lack of Confidence features may include pale eye color, a narrow face or jaw, fine eyebrows, unusual ear shapes, or a receding chin.

"Can I Change?"
Are the Psychological Meanings of Facial Features Fatalistic?

In the early books on Physiognomy written since 1800, the concept of facial features is taken very seriously – even to the degree of believing that they determine one's destiny. One book said that a mole on the tip of a narrow chin means you will be lonely and abandoned in old age. When I read this, my inner spirit rebelled. Not only did I find fatalistic pronouncements for someone's future depressing, but I wondered: "Is this accurate? Is there any hope of avoiding lonely destitution for this person?" I felt this fatalistic view did not take into account the possibilities for his healing – teachers or mentors who could model loving and positive relationships, travel or life experiences that could broaden his awareness, loving friends who could encourage him and be close even into old age. Unlike a black/white attitude my belief is that anyone can change if he wishes to. Take introspection, add dynamic will power, sprinkle in soul force, and anyone can remake his personality.

The goal is to understand the psychological meanings of your facial features, then to move beyond them!

Eye colors reflect specific emotional challenges

People who have these tell me they are learning to:
- Brown: not take things so personally
- Gray: increase their personal warmth in relationships
- Hazel: be calmer emotionally
- Blue/Gray: turn off their mind from over-analyzing

ᴅᴀᴛɪɴɢ

Where would you expect to find this person at a party?

1. In the corner under the fern reading a book

2. On the table in the middle of the room, telling jokes to the group

3. In the kitchen discussing German philosophers with the cook

Character analysis: This affectionate and friendly (wide mouth) person is very people oriented (lower lid being rounded) and fun loving (curly hair). He enjoys large parties and probably will be the center of attention.

Answer: (2)

CAREER

Which is the best job for this person?

1. A car mechanic who loves working along with machinery

2. A public relations specialist

3. A forest ranger who sits in a tower watching for summer fires

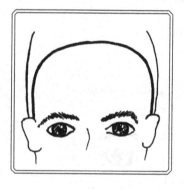 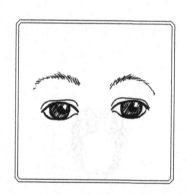 

Character analysis: A people-person from the start, this person has a gift for tact and friendship (rounded hairline) is generous (large eyes) and rounded eyebrows. He will be able to handle difficult people and challenging problems with warmth and sincerity.

Answer: (2)

Marriage

What will be the hardest adjustment area for him in an on-going intimate relationship?

1. Career choices and work

2. Sex and physical closeness

3. Budgeting and money problems

Character Analysis: Each of these three features express an easy, open style with spending money – maybe too easy. Budgeting will be a challenge for him as "the money goes in; the money goes out."

Answer: (3)

Shopping

Where does she shop?

1. A thrift store – always a bargain!

2. An expensive clothiers

3. A toy store

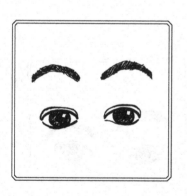
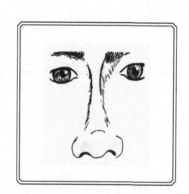

Character Analysis: The refinement (high eyebrows) and the fine hair suggest an intelligent person who is looking for value in things. The narrow nose bridge is a perfectionist. This person would make a good buyer for Nordstroms or a prestigious art gallery.

Answer: (2)

THREE SECTIONS OF THE FACE

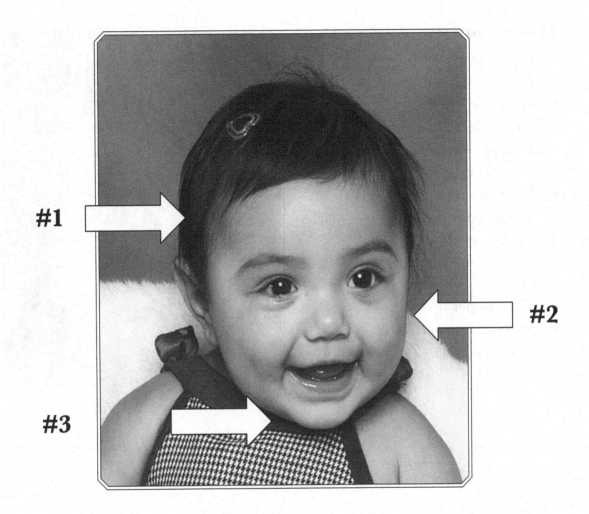

Section #1: Thinking Patterns
Forehead to the Eyebrows

Section #2: Emotional Responses
Eyebrows to the Mouth

Section #3: Will Power Area
Chin to the Jaw

Fran

Major Features:

- Fine hair
- Blue eyes
- Dimples
- Crow's feet
- Round chin
- "Teacher lines"
- Wide-set eyes
- Large front teeth
- Arched eyebrows
- Naso-labial lines around mouth
- Thin upper lip
- Vertical line across the nose bridge

Character Analysis:

Fran is vivacious, fun loving and has a great sense of humor. (dimples, crow's feet). She has a love for children and animals (rounded chin) and is well loved by her children and grandchildren. Her blue, clear eyes radiate understanding and wisdom. She can be dynamic and firm in her decisions (forward chin and large front teeth.) She has a gift for making everyone feel at home (naso-labial lines and round cheeks.) Fran has an eye for beauty (fine hair, arched eyebrows) and enjoys cultural events (arched eyebrow, crow's feet, "teacher lines"). Occasionally, she can become impatient (horizontal line across the nose), but she focuses on the Big Picture and the positive in others. She is definitely someone you want as a teacher or a Mom!

TASHA

Major Features:

- Rounded forehead
- Arched eyebrows
- Visible gums
- Ball on tip of nose
- Rounded chin
- Large front teeth
- Rounded cheeks
- Flat lower area (eye)
- Long earlobe
- Low-set ears

Character Analysis:

Tasha is a Queen of Hearts. Giving and being supportive of others comes naturally to her (rounded cheeks and round forehead.) Her nature is spiritual (long earlobes) and enthusiastic (radiant eyes). Tasha is a people person and the center of news, information and gossip (ball on tip of nose and round forehead). She will be a tremendous mom (forehead wispy corners and round chin). With all the positive indications for love and caring for others, the flat lower eye area gives her emotional grounding. An extrovert by nature, she needs to make sure she gets enough rest.

MIKE

Major Features:

- Wide-set eyes
- Huge jaw
- Forward chin
- Rounded cheeks
- Naso-labial lines
- Visible eyelids
- Low-set ears
- Curly hair
- Inner ear protrudes out
- Visible gums
- Large front teeth
- Dimples

Character Analysis:

Mike is dynamic, athletic, and action oriented (visible eyelids, huge jaw, and forward chin). Financially generous and someone who sees the Big Picture (visible gum line with round cheeks and wide-set eyes), he is a visionary by nature (inner ears protrude out). His dimples, curly hair, and radiant eyes reveal his great sense of humor and fun. Interested in humanitarian projects (high forehead with round cheeks), his greatest challenge is being patient with petty details and people who are not in integrity. His greatness will come forward after his mid-thirties (low-set ears).

PRACTICE
You In Different Stages of Life

Baby Photo	Toddler Photo	Grade School Photo	High School Photo	Young Adult Photo	Your Current Photo

Exercise: Find photos of these different phases of your life. Take out a sheet of paper. In each photo read the first five features you see and journal about what kind of person you were at that age. Reflect on what was happening for you at that time. What does each photo show about you? How are you evolving as a person?

Photos From Your Parents

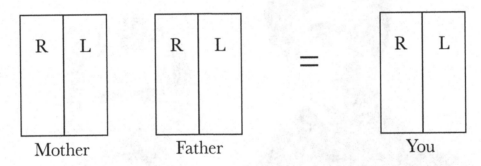

Compare the LEFT and RIGHT sides of your parents' faces. Then your face. How does your LEFT and RIGHT compare to their LEFT and RIGHT sides?

Reminder: In this technique you are looking for the feelings from one side of the face (not the facial features) as it compares to the other side.

Examples: Is the side of the face sad, happy, angry, frightened, joyful?

Left side: Personal, how he treats his family, how he feels about himself, his spiritual outlook, inner life, psychological recovery, inner transformation, is the glass "half empty or half full"?

Right side: Work life, outer life stressors (accidents, poverty, suffering, deaths), how people see him once he leaves his home in the morning, professional stressors or joys.

What does your face say you learned from them? What have you healed? What are you healing? Next, put your children's photos next to yours. Are there any family of origin issues that are being passed down from your parents to you and from you to your children? Do you like what you see?

WHAT DO THESE MEN HAVE IN COMMON?

Felix Kirk Zolliscoffer
American Confederate
Military Officer
1812-62

Edgar Allan Poe
American Poet & Writer
1809-49

Don Carlos I
Pretender to the Throne of Spain
1788-1855

John George Lambton
Governor General of Canada
1792-1840

Russell Alexander Alger
American Secretary of War
1836-1907

ANSWER: Triangle face shape – The forehead is the widest and chin is the apex. The meaning is someone who thinks fast, moves fast, and can be impatient. This is the best feature for writers or soldiers.

IS HE A MAN OF COMPASSION?
OR A MAN OF BITTERNESS?

William Tecumseh Sherman,
American Civil War General, 1820-91

ANSWER: Angular features (nose, huge jaw), tight mouth, hard eye tone, flat or tight cheeks. Man of bitterness. (As these drawings are not photos, so we are looking at the person through the artist's perception. This particular drawing follows this officer's battle in the Civil War, a historical-emotional moment of frustration.)

WHAT FEATURES DO THEY ALL SHARE?

Lord Derby
British Statesman
1799-1869

Nelson Appleton Miles
American General
1839-1925

Arnold Douglas
ator from Illinois
1813-61

Napoleon III
Emperor of France
1808-73

Alphonse de Lamartine
French Poet
1790-1869

George S. Boutwell
U.S. Secretary of the Treasury
1818-1905

ANSWER: They all have low-set ears meaning that they came into their success (family, money, happiness, career) in the second half of life (or somewhere between ages 35-50 in our current century). Also, they all have high foreheads (thinkers).

Actresses

Julia Marlowe
(stage name of Sarah Frances Frost)
American Actress

Cora Urquhart Potter
English-American Actress
1858-1936

Clara Louisa Kellogg
American Soprano
1842-1916

Left:

Cleft chin and large eyes show a playful, sentimental spirit

Middle:

Small mouth (which means rich fantasy life) and is the best feature for an actress

Right:

Ears that go out is the best feature for musical ability

WHAT ARE THE FIRST FIVE FEATURES YOU SEE?

Answer:

- Round hairline
- Narrow nose bridge
- Low-set eyebrows
- Flat cheeks
- Narrow face

Answer:

- Bushy eyebrows
- Low-set eyebrows
- Deep-set eyes
- Long earlobes
- Hawk nose

WHAT KIND OF LOVER IS HE?

Ferdinand
Duke of Orléans
1810-42

ANSWER: Sensual, passionate, and self-absorbed. High round forehead shows him to be a people person, yet the very small ears show him to be someone who would have difficulty understanding intimate communications. (His lover says "abc," he hears "kpf.") The sensuality is expressed in the dimpled chin and the triangle shaped face, but his very small mouth indicates he might have been selfish. He would be intensely passionate but emotionally confusing.

WHAT ARE THE FIRST FIVE FEATURES YOU SEE?

How do they relate to his life work?

John James Audubon
1785-1851

ANSWER: Low-set ears, large eyes, visible eyelids, large nose, forward chin, rounded eyebrows, large jaw, thick hair. John Audubon, an artist who studied birds and categorized them, had a balance of feeling (large eyes, rounded eyebrows) with a dynamic will (forward chin, large jaw). The thick hair reflects his love of the outdoors. So we see a naturalist with an appreciation for beauty.

WHAT WAS HE LIKE AS A COMMANDER?

George Henry Thomas
American Civil War General
1816-70

ANSWER: Forward jaw, forward chin, horizontal line across the nose (New feature! It means angry OR can be an expert in his career), two vertical lines into the forehead, tight mouth, small eyes, thin mouth, strong horizontal lines across forehead, intense low-set eyebrows. Leader? "Don't mess with me." Dynamic, angry, no nonsense, severe. Following rules and regulations was key.

COULD THIS POLITICIAN BE TRUSTED?

Wilfred Laurier
Canadian Statesman
1841-1919

ANSWER: Round, tall forehead, low-set eyebrows, low-set ears, a long philtrum (new feature! It is the area between the nose to upper lip is heavily grooved, meaning strong energy and life force to accomplish goals), wide cheeks (new feature! It means confident and responsible), short chin (new feature! May have some area related to "will power" and his body that is challenging for him. Examples: someone who is a picky eater, someone who hates taking care of his teeth), strong naso-labial lines that wrap around the mouth, flat cheeks. His flat lower lids indicate that he was cautious. Answer: YES! A confident and energetic leader, he could talk to anyone about anything. Definitely a people person, he was responsible and serious. He kept confidences well and performed his duties thoroughly, but with his flat cheeks he probably lacked a sense of fun and humor.

WAS HE A GOOD POPE? OR A BAD POPE?

ANSWER: A kind people person, he was a good communicator (naso-labial lines and rounded forehead, rounded chin). Low-set ears may indicate that he probably became Pope later in his life ("late bloomer"). His large nose is good for "abundance" whether that be spiritual or financial. His thin upper lip means he was good with in keeping confidences, an important character asset for a counselor or clergy member. Low-set eyebrows indicate a friendly person, someone others find easy to talk with. The strong, even and parallel lines in his forehead reveal a logical thinker and a good leader.

HOW DO THEIR FACES COMPARE?

Rugged Sportsmen

Pierre Lorillard
American Merchant & Sportsman
1833-1901

Albert Goodwill Spalding
American Athlete, Manufacturer
& Editor

Author of Children's Books

Hans Christian Andersen
Danish Story-writer
1805-75

ANSWER: Notice how the athlete's faces are angular and the jaws are wide. Force and dynamic energy are expressed. The author in the lower photo has many areas of rounding (forehead, cheeks, chin, lower area of eyes and eyebrows) expressing a gentle nature.

DO THESE MEN HAVE ANYTHING IN COMMON?

Cyrus West Field
American Financier

Cornelius Vanderbilt II
American Millionaire

ANSWER: Both have money noses/large noses and were very wealthy in the emerging industrial America.

WOULD YOU WANT HIM AS YOUR FATHER?

Charles Dickens

ANSWER: YES! He is interested in children (rounded chin), large inner hole inside ear (new feature! Means person has warm feelings), he enjoys peace and harmony at home (rounded eyebrows). Bright, inquisitive eyes also reflect kindness.

ROMANCE
How to Choose Your Soul Mate

All life involves understanding others. Our personal success and happiness depend on it. Face reading gives us the inner track in relationships. It looks at the core of a person and tells us who he really is. If he is a client, we can meet his unspoken needs with dynamic service which is tailored to him. If he is a child, we can help him cultivate and maximize his untapped, inner gifts. If he is a spouse or family member, face reading makes it easier to appreciate his strengths and to let go of unrealistic expectations. Only then can we grow closer in a real way.

Face reading offers a unique skill to help us in the area of romance and relationships. We want a match who will understand us mentally, physically, emotionally, and spiritually. We look for flowing, playful, natural harmony. What better way then to look for a mate who has similar facial features to ours? In other words, his natural range of behavior is compatible with ours. There is no stress or tension or bargaining when two people have the same energy patterns.

Because face reading focuses on facial features, which are universal for all ethnic groups, ages, and genders, two people can be romantically compatible even though they come from different continents or ethnic backgrounds. The key is that their facial features are similar. For intimate relationships to be lasting and harmonious, 70% of the facial features for a couple must match or be similar. Would this get boring to have someone whose inner flow is like ours? No. That is where the 30% difference in the facial features comes in. It adds the spark or chemistry.

What are "matching" or "similar" Facial Features?

1. *Facial Features are exactly the same.*
   Both people have black hair or visible eyelids or square foreheads.

2. *The eye colors are of the same intensity of color.*
   One has deep brown eyes, and the other has deep hazel eyes. One has light blue eyes, and other has light green eyes.

3. *The majority of the shapes of the features are similar.*
   Both have feeling predominant in their faces: rounded foreheads, round lower eye areas, and full cheeks. Both have physical or angular features: huge jaws, arched eyebrows and high cheek bones. Both have sensitive features: narrow faces, fine bone structure, and close set eyes.

4. *The textures in their features are the same.*
   Both have thick hair and eyebrows. Both have curly hair.

5. *The radiance from the eyes is the same.*
   Eye radiance is the degree of warmth, compassion, and love that radiates from a person's eyes. It is the barometer for soul development.

Once on TV the news anchor, Laura Buxton, asked me, "Will an Old Soul be happy in marriage with a Young Soul?" My response was what they want out of life and what they need to be happy is so very different that it is improbable. The Old Soul (whose eyes have radiance) wants to challenge and to develop his character – to change emotionally, spiritually or mentally for the better. He welcomes inner discovery and increasing awareness. A Young Soul (whose eye tone is flat, cold or even malicious) may be childlike in a playful way, self-absorbed or even dangerous. These people need tight rules and regulations to feel secure. What interests the two soul types is different so their needs in an intimate relationship will be different.

PUTTING IT ALL TOGETHER
The Worksheet for Compatibility

Using the following chart, compare you and your partner for compatibility.

Name: _____

Partner's Name: _____

Facial Features	We are the Same	We are Different
1) 3 AREAS OF THE FACE (which is biggest area of your face? Of your partner's face?)		
Forehead (intellectual)		
Cheeks (emotional)		
Jaw (will)		
2) HAIR		
Color (black, blond, brown, red)		
Texture (fine, thick)		
Type (curly, straight)		
3) UPPER FOREHEAD		
Shape (square, round, widow's peak, uneven, wispy)		
Height (tall/big, short)		
Lines (one/two vertical, three horizontal)		
4) EYES		
Color (blue, blue/gray, brown, gray, green, hazel)		
Size (large, small, right eye bigger, left eye bigger)		
Distance Between (wide-set, close-set)		
Eyelids (visible, non-visible)		
Area around Eyes (flat under, round under, "teacher lines", grief bags)		
Eyebrows Shape (thick, thin, arched, round, flat, uneven)		
5) CHEEKS		
Shape (high, flat, round)		
6) NOSE		
Shapes (large, hawk, broken/ages)		
Nostrils (visible, ball on tip)		
7) LIPS + MOUTH		
Lip Shape (full, thin, upper lip bigger, lower lip bigger)		
Mouth Size (large, small)		
8) TEETH		
Types (space in between front, large front teeth, small, chaotic)		
9) CHIN		
Shape (round, square, forward, dimple)		
10) JAW		
Shapes (large, narrow, left side bigger)		

WHERE INNER AND OUTER CHALLENGES SHOW IN THE FACE

Personal challenges come to us all. In our outer life we experience them in the form of problems with money, housing, health, jobs, education, family life, relationships, or legal issues. Inner challenges come in the form of feelings – fear, worry, loneliness, depression, hurt, anger, or frustration.

Unraveling the Meanings for the Two Sides of the Face

Exercise – How to do: use a blank sheet of white paper to do this. Hold it vertically so it covers one eye and half of the nose and mouth at the same time. In this particular exercise we do not look at individual the facial features. Instead, we focus on the feelings (joy, anger, fear, sadness, love) that come from both sides of the face and compare them.

The Right side of the face is reflective of our world interface – how we are in our jobs, how we connect to people once we leave our homes in the morning, our family of origin, what we see in our work (i.e., nurses who work with hospice see more suffering and death than mechanical engineers), outer stressors that change us (losing a job, illness, financial hardships, lawsuits).

The Left side of the face is reflective of our inner world – who we are when no one is looking, our innermost thoughts and feelings, our psychological resilience and spiritual transformation, and our inner joy or lack of it.

Though we cannot always change things that happen to us (our Right side), we can choose our attitude about how we will respond to them (our Left side.)

Three Options – Which are you?

- **The Left and Right sides are identical** in the feelings they radiate. What this means for the person is: "What you see is what you get." His personal and outer life are the same. No surprises here.

- **The Left side looks joyful, happy, or loving, and the Right side looks worried, tired, or angry.** This is not unusual in individuals who work in medicine or trauma (police, nurses, doctors, and therapists) as their jobs interface with death and suffering constantly. The Left side looks positive for them as often successful people in these occupations have an inner humanistic or spiritual/religious framework that helps them to mentally and emotionally cope with their work.

- **The Right side of the face shows positive emotions, but the Left side looks disturbed, fearful, or angry.** This means that the individual is privately coping with inner battles, worries, or stressors. Or this might indicate a darker, unconscious side to this person, which may come up in how he treats his wife or children. If the left side appears cruel or cold, look at other photos of the same person. If this is a consistent pattern, he may be unaware of how is negative behavior is hurting others.

Your Notes:

HEALTH OR ILLNESS?
FACIAL INDICATORS

The body is always recording what is happening to us. Just as we look at our dog's coat as an indicator of his general health, there are facial indicators which also give information about our health and wellness. From traditional physiognomy, the following are examples of some of the indicators for health and long life: (And yes, you can be healthy and well without having any of them!)

- Eyes which have radiance, or energy, or emotional warmth
- Philtrum (the area from the nose tip to the upper lip) is vertically marked with a strong line
- Nose bridge is broad, and there are no breaks along the nose
- Chin is broad and comes forward and is without cleft or dimple
- A wide chin indicates dynamic physical endurance while a narrow chin may denote uneven patterns of physical energy during the day
- Ears have a rounded upper rim and a long earlobe. Ears are thick and strong
- Skin is clear and free from scarring

The following features are generalities, but may indicate the beginning of possible health concerns:

- Dark blue shadows under eyes = allergies or sensitivity to perfume, paint and/or smoke
- Vertical parallel lines above upper lip (found in people who were past smokers) = may have digestive problems
- Red Nose = hypoglycemia (low-blood sugar)
- Eyebrows (thinning of outer 1/3 nearest to ear, if not related to eyebrow plucking) = slow thyroid function
- Ear, diagonal crease across the lobe (only) = family history of heart problems (For example, that would mean strokes, heart attacks, high blood pressure, or anemia in parents or grandparents)
- Small pores + fine hair + delicate bone structure = may have hypoglycemia (low blood sugar)

- Women only: horizontal line above the top lip = irregular menstrual periods, possible infertility. Mole above or to outside of outer upper lip = possible menstrual problems
- Men, balding in crown area (top of) head = possible cardiac (heart) problems after age 40

Reminder: Face reading does not medically diagnose. It is not a replacement for medical or psychiatric evaluation and treatment. If you have any health concerns, please see your doctor for an evaluation.

BUSINESS AND MANAGEMENT
How to Read Your Employee's (or Boss's) Face

The following facial features will tell a manager how his employee will:

- Interact with other team members

- Approach a new project

- Adhere to company's guidelines

- Be able to work independently

- Best be guided by you

Note: Although there are thousands of facial features, some will impact business and work more than others. Those are the ones I've chosen below. Do remember to combine all the features to make a complete character analysis of a person.

Eyes
An employee's vision, attention to details, ability to concentrate on projects

CLOSE-SET EYES

Employee on the Job:
Perfectionist, precision oriented, loves details, introvert, and good concentration on projects.

How to guide him:
Analyze the project in parts giving full explanation of whys and wherefores that might come up in writing his documentation. Give him 10 minutes of your overall vision so he gets the understanding of how to format the pieces. Let him work independently and report back to you. Let him know which parts of the puzzle are important/or not.

WIDE SET EYES

Employee on the Job:
Will understand and appreciate your vision for the team, company or project. May be late for meetings. May procrastinate on deadlines. Not as attentive with details.

How to guide him:
He can do great PR work and is an excellent fund raiser or morale booster. Make sure he documents his time and stays focused by reporting on project developments. Talk over your vision for the company with him and brain storm project ideas. He'll have many.

Eyebrows

*Personal power, how he will set up the project,
his anger-animation-energy in team meetings*

VISIBLE EYELIDS

Employee on the Job:

"Give it to me; I'll do it." Action oriented doer. Good with deadlines, organized.

How to guide him:

Make sure he understands your wishes before he moves into dynamic action. It's hard to slow down a tornado once it's in movement. He might not understand the importance of research and development as he puts more emphasis on action. Not being attached to the results of the project (whether it succeeds or fails) is a lesson for him in detachment. Encourage him to be doing his very best regardless.

NON-VISIBLE EYELIDS

Employee on the Job:

List maker, sets up systems for others to follow, thinks through projects.

How to guide him:

Give him time to set up a system for the company. Whatever the department, he's your time management person. Perfect for a dispatcher job or a RN public health nurse who sets up the medical plan for team members to follow. Make sure that you have problem solved areas of emotional, political or logistic difficulties before the new system is implemented.

ARCHED EYEBROWS

Employee on the job:

Gifted in drama, loves cultural events and the arts. Has flair for color, fabric and texture. Can be either great mentor but if dissatisfied, can stir up the Team. Powerful for good or bad.

How to guide him:

Have him mentor creative, bright new employees. He's the one to set up company Christmas parties or entertain out of town clients. If he starts to verbalize problems, take time to listen. Anything related to office design, he's your perfect person for the job.

ROUNDED EYEBROWS

Employee on the job:

Peace maker, wants Team harmony and is concerned for other's feelings, warm.

How to guide him:

Appreciate his genuineness and desire to have Team members happy. He's your barometer for the company's inner emotional pulse. Pay attention. Spend 5 minutes a day at his desk. The personal warmth you show him will be passed on to others, and he will go a long way to represent your interests where you are not present at the office. Let him be in charge of Xmas gifts, cards, birthdays.

FRIENDLINESS

LOW-SET EYEBROWS

Employee at job:

Friendly, able to put others at ease quickly, approachable for clients.

How to guide him:

Send him out to work with difficult clients or to entertain clients from out of town. He's great with children, grandparents and can charm anyone. Best person to welcome new employees or listen to complaints and smooth things over for you. Great at PR or HR (all those R's). If he wants to become too familiar, be friendly but have firm emotional boundaries.

HIGH-SET EYEBROWS

Employee on the job:

High standards, not easily impressed by other people, socially selective, may be at times reserved with other employees.

How to guide him:

Quality control is his middle name. Let him use his white gloves on everything. He'll do it anyway, so you might as well value his gift for seeing flaws. Do not put him in social settings. Let him work independently and report back to you. Can be a bit aloof. Remind him that he is part of a team lest others think him arrogant (instead of a loner).

PHYSICAL ENDURANCE ON THE JOB

FINE EYEBROWS

Employee on the Job:

Sensitive, gentle with the feelings of others, may physically tire easily (needs breaks after 5-6 hours of intense work), tactful, sweet, can be high strung if tired.

How to guide him:

Wrong person to handle angry clients. (Will burn him out for days!) Has velvet gloves to handle clients and be charming. Do not put him to long work days. If you walk by his desk and he's playing solitaire on the computer, ignore it. He's recharging his mental batteries (unless he's always playing solitaire!)

THICK EYEBROWS

Employee on the job:

He'll be there 7 AM to 7 PM, forceful in his opinions, has leadership qualities.

How to guide him:

Remind him to go home to his family at night. That is OK. Teach him to step down his emotional intensity with other team members. Not everything needs to be handled at 60 M.P.H. Put him at the head of a project whenever possible. Other team members will automatically take direction from him. Unless he's arrogant or has his own agenda, and then be very careful.

EDITOR LINES AND SENSE OF HUMOR

DOWNWARD LINES ONTO OUTER CHEEK AREA

Employee on the job:

Excellent teacher, writer or speaker, good with grammar and vocabulary.

How to guide him:

Let him proof read any company documents and papers. Send him to give all your the classes and lectures. He will be patient with customers helping them with complicated equipment. If he corrects your grammar, be grateful he's paying attention to your stories. Great person to write the company manual.

CROW'S FEET (LINES GO UP AT EYE CORNERS)

Employee on the job:

Loves to make people laugh, playful and fun. Can lighten up dull staff meetings.

How to guide him:

Appreciate his sense of lightness. It might come in handy with an angry board member or disgruntled client or in a Staff meeting where everyone is sleeping. The day goes by more easily with humor. Great person to tell your fishing stores to. You definitely want him to write your speeches.

NOSE

Independent worker or social team member

NARROW NOSE BRIDGE

Employee on the job:

Perfectionist, functions well independently, great at quality control.

How to guide him:

Remind him it's OK to make mistakes and to learn from them. Help him to emotionally and socially integrate into the team as he might be a bit of a loner. (Greta Garbo) Can be a bit eccentric at times (Prince Charles). He loves classical string instruments so get him a guitar or string CD for Christmas. Appreciate his delicate sensitivity unless he's being a bore or inappropriate.

ROUND BALL ON NOSE TIP

Employee on the job:

Center of news, information and gossip. People tell them everything!

How to guide him:

Make sure the gossip in the office isn't about you! Limit the personal information you give him, but listen if he tells you the scoop on clients. He knows the truth of all. Encourage confidentiality in him. He'd be good as a scout behind enemy lines in a war. He'll enjoy doing research on the internet for projects. (R&D) If he's wasting time, move his desk away from the water cooler.

MOUTH

Degree of personal warmth with clients and team members

SMALL MOUTH (TINY)

Employee on the Job:

Introvert, may be self-absorbed, rich fantasy life.

How to guide him:

Great for actor or the arts. May have own agenda. Listen if he verbalizes unhappiness. Introvert. Help him to reach out to other team members and see other's points of view. He'll want to work independently. See if that meets your project's needs. Encourage him to be more generous with information and ideas.

WIDE MOUTH (LARGE)

Employee on the Job:

Generous, big spirited, great teacher, sales and PR is his middle name.

How to guide him:

Put him in charge of welcoming new clients or employees and making them feel at home. He will frequently shake your hand or reach out to hug other team members. That's good. It means he's in his element and happy. Difficult clients will love him. Make sure he's not giving too much away $$ in the product agreements and promises to clients. Help him to not take everything personally.

THIN LIPS

Employee on the Job:

Very business like, can be terse, not a people person but more of a technician, private, non-emotional.

How to guide him:

If he can work independently on the project and report back to you, that's the best. Other team members might find him downright annoying or lacking personal warmth. Help him to understand that other's emotions matter just as much as "getting the job done."

LARGE FRONT TEETH

Employee on the Job:

Determined, can be stubborn where it matters, strong willed, no wimp here!

How to guide him:

Make sure he understands what you want and what is important in each project before he puts on his Crusades' cape for you. Also, with strong determination and will that are natural to him, make sure he checks in with you every few days to make sure he's doing the project along the format you wish.

JAW AND CHIN

Degree of assertiveness in the world of business

NARROW JAW

Employee on the job:

Gifted but shy, not good at marketing himself, gentle, poor physical endurance for long work days.

How to guide him:

Don't underestimate his quietness for lack of competence. "Still waters run deep." Lincoln had this face shape. Great person to understand the depth of other's feelings and also their hidden motives. If he's self-employed, you handle his marketing for him. May not be assertive, but neither is he passive. Not good with argumentative clients.

WIDE JAW

Employee on the job:

Strong physical endurance, can work long hours without breaks, takes command, forceful, willful, and dynamic.

How to guide him:

Put him in command – He'll get there anyway on his own. Needs to be in charge or will stir up mischief. Great in outdoor physical jobs. Can lift tall buildings with a single hand. Admire and appreciate his stamina for the company. Exudes authority and is good person to represent you in negotiations or meetings. Can be overbearing at times.

FORWARD CHIN (PROFILE)

Employee on the job:

Moves forward on projects, goes past all obstacles, eats problems for breakfast.

How to guide him:

Remind him to check in with you – that you are the boss. Give him free reign once you trust him. Naturally confident, he can be fearless. Makes a good mentor for more timid employees. Good morale builder. Remind him that not everyone is as forthright as he is – that others may need to take more time to develop their plan of action. (If he also has visible eyelids, he moves at warp speed. Make sure he takes Calcium to calm down.)

RECEDING CHIN (PROFILE)

Employee on the job:

May be timid or shy. Probably abhors direct confrontations or speaking up for himself. Needs to learn assertiveness.

How to guide him:

Great facial feature for jobs requiring gentleness (dog trainer, child care) – miserable feature for tasks involving extroverted, confident stance. If you are patient in helping him build his self-esteem, he will admire you and never forget you. Be his advocate in difficult negotiations so he can learn how to do these maneuvers. It'll pay off later.

THE JOB YOU WERE BORN TO DO!

Below are patterns of facial features found in people who are successful and happy in these careers:

Analytical, Computer, Technical, or Mechanical Jobs

- Blue-Gray Eyes = analytical, systems oriented, left brained profession

- Non-visible Eyelids = sets up systems for others to follow, list maker, planner

- Close-set Eyes = detail, precision oriented, focused, good at research projects

- Gray Eye Color = private, non-emotional, able to examine details, detached

- Narrow Nose Bridge = perfectionist, high standards, aristocratic

- Large, Wide Forehead = thinker, strategist, planner, mental focus

- Small Eye Size = aware of all details around them, sees everything, loves details

- High Eyebrows = high standards, not easily impressed by others, very loyal to friends even though very selective

Artistic, Musical, or Design Jobs

- Thin, long ears = good with texture, fabric and color, advertising, merchandising and interior design, or hair color

- Widow's Peak = artistic, creative, individualist, likes to dress casually and be his own boss

- Fine Hair = sensitive, very aware of environment (emotional or physical) or needs of others

- Fine Skin Pores (cheek) = chooses expensive items, great taste in shopping, sensitive, refined

- Ears Come Forward = music ability, sensitive to vibration and sound, individualist

- Small Mouth = rich fantasy life, artist

- Close-set Eyes = detail, precision oriented, great for composing music, focus to design a project

- Full, Large Mouth = affectionate, generous, passionate feelings, emotionally swayed

- Large Eyes = feeling oriented, big hearted, sensitive

Communication Jobs
Teacher, Minister, Counselor, or Writer

- Round Forehead Shape = people person, has many long-term friendships, enjoys communication

- Large Ears = listens well to others, tunes in to the Big picture, wants a win/win for everyone, sensitive

- Round Ball on Tip of Nose = center of news, information and gossip. People tell him everything! He remembers stories about people and their relatives.

- Hazel eyes = interest in healing and insight, loves multi-tasking and variety, takes self-development classes

- Lines Downward from Outer Eye = teacher, loves writing, teaching or speaking, has great grammar, probably speaks language(s)

- Crow's Feet = adds humor and fun to personal relationships, sunny disposition

- Thin Upper Lip/Large Lower Lip = keeps confidential information private and doesn't gossip

- High Placed Ears = excels academically, often has two college degrees, good memory, intelligent

- Large (Wide) Mouth = warm hearted, generous, affectionate

Physical or Outdoor Jobs: Fireman, Policeman, Personal Trainer, Gardener

- Thick Hair = love of the outdoors, physically resilient

- Deep (strong) Eye Color = If Blue (or Blue-Gray), he loves the ocean. If Hazel or Brown, he loves plants, flowers, and trees

- Philtrum (area between tip of nose and upper lip) is vertically grooved = strong life force or endurance

- Thick Eyebrows = strong life force, good ability to heal from illness, great physical energy and drive

- Full Thick Beard = robust, full of dynamic energy, enjoys physical work outdoors

- Large Jaw = willful, powerful to accomplish goals, loves to exercise and physically train

- Thick Eyebrows + Deep Vertical Line in Philtrum = strong constitution physically, great endurance

Sales, Marketing, or Insurance Jobs

- Round Forehead Shape = people person, love to take time to help others, friendship oriented

- Wide Mouth = generous, affectionate, warm hearted

- Ball on Tip of Nose = center of news, information and gossip, people tell them everything!

- Curved Lines (Pear shape) around the Mouth (Naso-labial lines) = He can talk to anyone about anything! Great communicator

- Face Shape is a Circle = (shape of a baby's face) People trust you and hand you money

- Wide Cheek Area (between Nose to Ear) = Confident, projects that he knows what he is doing at all times, responsible

- Jaw Projects Forward = Go getter, dynamic, eats problems for breakfast (lunch and dinner)

Your Notes:

DANGEROUS FACIAL FEATURES

How to Identify Them!

After 9-11 I worked on a project with the FAA to identify "dangerous" facial features. This was to be used by baggage-checkers and airport security. When the FAA was replaced by the TSA, my project and many others were discontinued due to finances. However, before that I had the opportunity to analyze and evaluate hundreds of photos of international felons, WWII spies, gangsters, Outlaws of the Old West, rapists, FBI most-wanted, and terrorists. Below are examples of patterns of dangerous facial features I saw in hundreds of criminal photos. Although it is my personal belief that anyone can change for the better, the more of these dangerous features a person has, the less likely he is to feel that he needs to change his deviant behavior. Combine these features below with a flat, cold or angry eye tone, and the criminal intention magnifies.

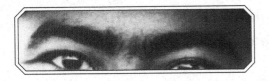

Unibrow - cruel

Eye Energy - suspicious and mean

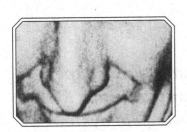

Hawk Nose - vicious, treacherous

> *Any man can change his character for the better, but the more of these "dangerous" features he has, the less he will feel he needs to change. He feels instead that he is a victim, and that life owes him whatever he can grab.*

 **Vacant Eyes**

Scary Eyes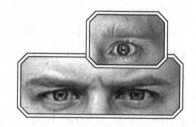

 **Eyes: White (Sclera) shows under Iris – emotionally unraveling, very dangerous, vicious (To see this: You must be on eye level with this person.)**

Sunken Cheeks: lack of loving and nurturing as a child, unable to give and receive warmth or affection

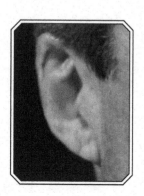     **Unusual Ear Shapes: major trauma(s) to the neurological system (emotions)**

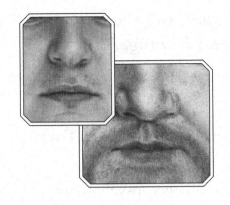

Small Mouth: (size of nose or smaller) self-absorbed, rich fantasy life, narcissistic

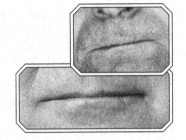

Tight, Thin Lips (all the time): angry, brutal, or aggressive

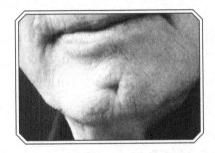

Dimple in Chin (donut): strong sensual drive/or passionate person. If combined with major violent features, this man could sexually mistreat women.

"Joker's" Mouth: (upper lip only, skin in outer edges presses down making the red part of lip very small) parents were controlling, critical or emotionally oppressive

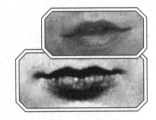

Clenched Jaw: rage

This book should be read by all in law enforcement. Barbara confirmed a theory I had always felt. I was astonished by the number of "truths."

— Andrew Van Wagenen, retired NY police officer (25 years)

"So my family wasn't the Mafia, but they weren't so great either. How will that show in my face? How can I change?"

In the 10,000 people whose faces I've read, only four have told me they were from "healthy, terrific families," and that their childhoods were wonderful.

(I like to joke that I had lunch with one of these mother-son families. And I'm not so sure about them! So that makes only three?)

In the last few years many doctors, parole and police officers, psychotherapists and psychiatrists have attended my classes. They have validated many of the following features from their case observations and clinical experience. When I showed one therapist a facial features found in men who sexually hurt women, she told me that she noticed this same feature "appeared consistently in her caseload of sexual perpetrators." One homicide detective told me, "I wish I had known about you and these 'dangerous features' when I was working the street! I had to figure this all out on my own."

If a person has one of two of the "challenging childhood" features, he might have had negative situations to overcome. However, when "dangerous" facial features show in multiple areas of the face, the indication is that the person had endured severe traumas growing up.

How do you explain the example of people who have had horrible childhoods, but this does not show in their facial features?

Even when clients tell me of severely abusive childhoods, those who have had loving or emotionally supportive connections outside of their home life (say, with a teacher, neighbor, grandparent, counselor, or spiritual guide) can have a face that shows only a minimal amount of trauma.

Reminder: Face Reading is not a replacement for professional counseling or medical diagnosis and intervention. It is an introspective tool, a way of reading the body's messages. Please refer to your own doctor or counselor for personal assessment and treatment.

Introspection is the first step to achieving personal greatness.

These are features found in clients who have had challenging childhoods:

- One front tooth crosses or blocks the other front tooth – a parent blocked their creativity in childhood
- Uneven forehead hairline (chaotic family) – their own emotional needs were unmet
- Mouth that is held tight – emotional rage or lack of personal warmth
- Flat, cold or angry eyes – distant emotionally or no conscience
- Patch mustache – (as seen in Hitler) - full of rage and paranoid
- Chaotic teeth – (teeth that cross over each other or go in different directions) – non-nurturing or chaotic childhood
- Horizontal line across the nose bridge – anger issues OR expert in their professional area
- Eye (White/Sclera completely surrounds the iris of the eye/colored area) – vicious and violent OR hyperthyroidism
- Crooked nose will indicate the age a person is when a major trauma(s) occurred. These major changes can be any of the following: divorce, bankruptcy, death of loved one, moving across the country, return to school/end of school, ill heath.
- Eyebrows angle (form a inverted "V" over the eye, with the highest arch being above the pupil area or both angle down from the temples to point towards ears – can be volatile or dynamic
- Small ears (as compared to the overall proportional size of the face) – doesn't understand verbal communication. You say "abc" and they hear "kmp."
- Short forehead (the distance between the eyebrows and the hairline is short relative to the shape of the whole face) – impulsive, doesn't think through consequences of his actions
- Bottom 1/3 of the face (from the mouth to the jaw area) is very short or tiny compared to the length of the face – poor impulse control
- Left eye wanders, away from the center (IF not strabismus or lack of physical eye muscle control) – may be self-sabotaging
- Left eye is lower than the right eye (if two are placed on a horizontal line) – difficulty with the father – which means the father was away while the person was growing up, worked long hours, or there was divorce or a physical separation. The degree of emotional distance is related to how much lower the left eye is in relation to the right one
- Eyes that appear slit like (when the person is smiling, but not looking at the sun) – emotionally removed or distant, not focused on the material world

WHAT YOUR OWN FACE REVEALS

Eye Radiance

Before studying face reading, we are used to looking at people without really seeing them. After studying this, we not only understand them, but we know more about ourselves as well. We may wish to have features which indicate more health, wealth, or fame. And like others we see, our own emotional, spiritual, and physical development takes time. Our face will change as we do meditative or psychological work to free ourselves from self-doubt, pain, fear, or self-limitations.

Of all the facial features, the eye radiance shows emotional recovery and spiritual transformation the clearest. People's eyes have a predominant emotion coming from them. It may be compassion (Christ), kindness (Martin Luther King), charisma (Elvis), intellect (Colin Powell), anger (McCarthy, the Communist hunter in the 1950s), meanness (Hitler), sensuality (Catherine Zeta-Jones).

If a person's eyes radiate compassion, wisdom, love or joy, then even if all the facial features appear negative, they are making spiritual progress despite obstacles. What separates the faces of saints from criminals? Both may have "negative" facial features which reveal severe personal trauma. However, the saintly person has radiance and love pouring from their gaze. The criminal's eyes are flat, vicious or cold.

Radiance in a person's eye tone means the following emotionally:

- He is aware of his psychological shortcomings or life lessons and wishes to work through them, instead of ignoring or denying them.

- He is actively working these shortcomings out.

- He has finished working them out.

Radiance emanating from the eyes indicates the person is living more from their soul nature and less from his psychological personality.

Long ago an emperor wanted a painting of the most famous prophet in his realm. He commissioned his best painter to complete the work, and shortly after the oil painting was unveiled before the whole court. Understanding physiognomy, the Emperor became confused as he looked at the painting. The facial features of the prophet revealed not a great soul but a man of evil nature. Taking the whole court with him, the monarch went on horseback to meet this man. On seeing the prophet's face the monarch was astounded to realize that the art work had been a perfect rendering.

"Well, the physiognomy experts must be useless men," the Emperor thought.

The wise one, who understood the monarch's dilemma explained, "Physiognomy is a true science. All my facial features did express my past evil tendencies, but one by one I have battled against these defects of character. I have transformed each evil into good, and that is what has given me my Inner power."

The difference between a criminal and a saint is the energy radiating from the eyes. If there is radiance (warmth, feeling, depth, compassion) coming from the eyes, then that person may be psychologically/spiritual developed despite facial features that indicate a traumatic childhood or circumstances. One example is a Canadian saint named Brother Andre. A humble monk who was the porter for his monastery, he would heal the sick who came to the Church. The walls of St. Joseph's Church where he is buried are lined with hundreds of feet of real crutches and bandages of those he healed. Photos of his face showed features revealing many personal obstacles. Yet his eyes were radiant with the joy of God.

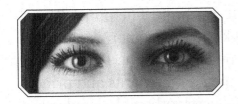

Alert

Compassionate

Loving

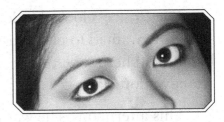

Thoughtful

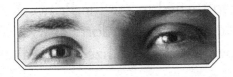

Laughing

FACE READING SHORT STORIES

———❀———

THE PRINCESS AND THE GARDENER

Alabaster straightened his legs and shook the dust from his hands. He was hidden behind the ferns in the fountain he was planting for the emperor. At one time he had been a brave knight leading troops into battle, but his face had been burned and scarred in one siege. So he wore a mask to cover his deformity so that he would not frighten the children and the women would not pity him. The court artist had woven the mask to resemble the face Alabaster had had before the burns. The king had given him the role of Royal Gardener for the palace. At least he was still useful to his to his liege, so he was happy.

His fingers went to rest on the hoe as he watched the scene at the far end of the courtyard. Princess Lisette was being led by her maid to a stone bench surrounded by his Glory roses. Her woven long hair was filled with sunshine. The pink silk and damask laced gown was the color of her blushing cheeks as each suitor approached her. The runners had spread the word through the provinces that the Princess was seeking a husband, so men – brave and tall, short and pudgy, merchants and princes came forward. Some of the knights boasted of their conquests, others flaunted velvet jackets and laced shirts. And some became mute when they saw her beauty. She regarded all with quiet humility. Princess Lisette listened, nodded and smiled. But she refused them all.

Her father, the king, paced before her seat, "Darling, you have to accept one of them! I need an heir. Please!"

Lisette replied, "Papa, I need to find someone I love. I refuse to marry someone I don't love." A similar discussion between them ensued week after week. The king would shake his head and pace with exasperated sighs.

The Princess looked forlorn. She was firm, but being loving and kind by nature, she really wanted to please her father. Alabaster noted with admiration her skin, her hands, and her modest smile. He had memorized each of her gowns and silently and secretly adored her.

This afternoon as he was planting the Glory red roses, he heard a quiet weeping coming from her direction. Immediately he stopped and turned to see the Princess sighing and softly dabbing her eyes with a lace clothe. He wanted to comfort her with all his heart but was hesitant as he was only the gardener. Then he realized the real reason was that he was ashamed of his facial burns and the mask he wore to cover them.

So he placed himself near her chair but remained hidden. "My lady, I am only the gardener, but I wish to know why you weep. Please tell me the reason for your sadness."

Princes Lisette turned to the area of the ferns to see a tall and muscular man in simple garb. His hands were large and strong, but his face was obscured by the foliage.

"Sir, for weeks my father, the King, has been trying to find a suitor for my hand in marriage. Though many men have come to me, none of them move my heart." She inhaled a sob.

Alabaster's facial burns had deepened his sensitivity to other's sorrows and unfulfilled longings. In his heart he had lived a million lives in his one body, and his heart had seen and touched them all.

"My lady," he began, "I understand the heart's longing for pure love. *Pure love alone can satisfy. Divine Love alone can heal. It is worth waiting for such a love.*"

Comforted that someone understood her inner feelings, the princess turned to him and asked, "And how is it a gardener speaks with such wisdom? Will you tell me your story and how you have come to know of such things?" And so began many conversations and a friendship between the two. Every week Alabaster would put a perfect Glory on her chair. His heart would quicken when he saw her satin gowns entering his floral cave. Sometimes they would talk between suitors. She understood his thoughts and shared his observations. And they laughed. Week after week his secret love for her grew.

"Love can heal. Love can change you. It is worth waiting for such a love."

By fall the leaves were red and yellow canopies above the alcove. All week he would go over the words he would say to her. He reviewed her mannerisms, her smiles. And even though he told her *"Love can heal,"* in his own heart, he knew she could never love him. His face was burned beyond recognition, and he was afraid to be seen without his mask.

The princes from the outlining provinces had come and gone on horseback. The king was going bald from tearing out his hair, and the Queen had stopped eating for her worry over Lisette. The Princess was given an ultimatum that she must choose a husband or be banished to the outer forest with her maid.

When Alabaster brought her morning beverage, Lisette spoke up, "My friend, we have spent months talking and coming to understand each other's inner hearts. I know you are noble and true. Your voice is the one I hear in my mind when I go to sleep and when I awaken at dawn. But Alabaster, I so long to see your face as it really is. Please show me."

The gardener was shocked by her request and felt deep sorrow. "Princess, what we have now must be enough. I cannot show you my face as in battle it was scarred and changed. I fear that if you really saw me, you would be horrified and banish me from your sight. My heart would break if I could not be your friend."

Lisette looked at him with a firm gaze, "I know who you are inside, Alabaster. That is enough for me. Please take off your mask so that my fingers might stroke your wounds and give you comfort. Your burns must make you feel lonely, and I seek to give back to you a portion of the love you have given me." And she became quiet and waited.

"Love can heal. Love can change you. It is worth waiting for such a love."

So for the first time since his battle, he reached for the artificial covering over his face and carefully removed the mask. He waited for her shock and horror. He waited for a gasp or scream. And nothing came. He looked up into her deep eyes to a smiling face.

"My beloved," she said lovingly, "Your face has become the same as the mask. *Love can heal. Love can change you. It is worth waiting for such a love.*"

To the joy of the king and all the land the Royal Gardener was wedded to the princess. The king got a wig. The country gave a huge banquet for the wedding, and the queen started eating again.

Abraham Lincoln Chooses His Cabinet

Abraham Lincoln emerged from the War Room tired and sick at heart. He had just come from the battlefield where he visited the tents of the surgeons. His mind held the continuous image of timelessly sobbing widows in long black dresses. Hopeless, orphaned sons and daughters cried at the doors of their homes waiting for fathers who would never return.

Although he had surrounded himself politically with those who had opposed him and wished for his nation to be open to all men and all views, the president was acutely aware that political incompetence meant wounded soldiers and dead men. His heart was filled with quiet grieving, and the Great War was never far from his heart for a moment.

"To even have a healthy son reach adulthood was a miracle of God," he reflected. "So many epidemics of flu or cases of consumption. Even a body soaked with rain on a wintry day might be lost by nightfall."

So that some of the city's young bucks dreamed of the "battle cry" and fighting to prove their manhood angered him deep in his soul. That the young people romanticized war gave him lingering sadness. If only they saw what he had seen: brothers in battle together, one kneeling over his dying loved one. And no grieving, they say, can compare to a parent who has lost a son. He had Todd, and he knew what the all encompassing love of a father could be – protective and tender at the same time.

And how cruel men and nature could be to the human flesh. Some was Fate. War was choice. He was determined to end the War as quickly as he could. Send just one son home to his Mama – one son who might never have had a chance on the battlefield. It would be worth one son – whole and well.

So much rested on the integrity and capabilities of the men he chose for his Cabinet. His leaders must be of the highest caliber. Strong, fearless and true. They must be understanding of his people, their children, and the future of a great nation. Everything was at stake now. Of the Cabinet he had chosen, some were from different states and had different backgrounds. He liked that about them. He chose them by looking closely at their military records, their letters of accommodation, and by reading their characters. He tried not to miss anything. As president he could not control much, but he could hand-select his men who would make national decisions. That was his job. The destiny of a nation at War depended on it. He must not fail his people.

When he was younger, the Illinois lawyer had met with one obstacle after another. Some eight at least, he reflected. Many elections lost. To others he seemed like a complete failure. But in each political skirmish he had learned to look at people closely and assess their nuances of personality. So their behavior or decisions would never surprise him. He knew more about some people than they knew about themselves, but he kept his own council. He studied the ancient system of physiognomy (face reading). Ten feet from a prospective juror or witness in a trial, he could turn the fate of a legal outcome. Lincoln could laugh and weave a good story with the best of them, but inside he had the instincts of a cougar. He looked at people and saw them – beyond artifices, fancy verbiage, and fine clothes. He would laugh at a child's story and shun an arrogant general.

One afternoon as his Cabinet assembled in the White House, the sun's hot fierceness poured through the room. Men were loosening their neck clothes and removing their bulky jackets, wiping their forehead with large white hankies. All stood as Lincoln entered the room. His hands rose palms down to motion them to be seated.

"I understand that today we are reviewing the application for Lt. James McNeed, who wishes to be Secretary of the Treasury. Will those of you who have letters of accommodation, military files and written testimonials about him, please step forward." Lincoln seated himself behind the mahogany desk and opened his right hand to receive the papers. Letters from Generals, teachers, red wax sealed missives about Lt. McNeed were handed over. The pile was so high that by the time Lincoln had read them all the sun was setting. The men were eager to get into their carriages and return home to their wives and dinners.

"Well," Lincoln began, "he seems an ideal candidate from these dossiers. His war record is impeccable, and I can find no fault with anything I have read about this man. Let us meet him now so we might to return to a quiet evening with our families. Bring Lt. James McNeed to me please."

The side door opened, and the attending army aide ushered a man in uniform into the room. He came to stand directly in front of Abraham Lincoln. The president's gaze was powerful and searching as he regarded the officer. Lincoln was reviewing McNeed's facial features, from a system called face reading. It helped him to accurately access a person's character. In his mind, Lincoln made note of McNeed's features: *a dimpled chin that was short, a chin which receded back to tuck behind forward thrusting front teeth, an uneven forehead hairline, a tiny, tight mouth (that looked like a man set on a vinegar drink), strange ears which protruded out from his head at odd angles, a mouth that upturned like a joker (but McNeed wasn't smiling), and a thick unibrow eyebrow.* The president reflected that he looked like a rat. And then Lincoln remembered the words of Aristotle, the first great scholar in the science of physiognomy: "If you look like an animal, you are it!"

(You will have the temperament of that animal.)

What was curious about McNeed, Lincoln thought, was that as he answered each direct question, his eyes would shift, almost retract visibly. Then, they would become clear and present. It seemed to happen when the questions involved his military record. Lincoln had learned to recognize this eye change as "cloaking," and he had seen it often in spies of all sorts. The president paced up and down, his head bowed, reflective before his men.

He made his decision and turned to the group, "Please leave us, Mr. McNeed."

And after the man disappeared down the corridor, Lincoln turned to the curious Cabinet members and said, "I don't want this man anywhere close to me." Lincoln pounded his open flat hand onto his desk as the astonished group gasped and was riveted to attention. "Show me a man who is forty who is not responsible for his face." With that he pulled in his vest and with long strides left the room.

Weeks later a news bulletin emerged from a Border state with an artist's rendering of an escaped convict, Walter McNeed, who had been incarcerated for killing his brother, Lt. James McNeed, and stealing his military papers. The murdered brother, Lt. James McNeed had been a valiant soldier, decorated in battle. And for those who studied the facial drawing closely, the man who had stood before Lincoln had been none other than Walter McNeed.

CHOOSING A MAN OF DESTINY

In a distant territory the elders of a court were gathered around the bed covers of their dying king. His elderly wife bathed his hands and gently massaged his feet to comfort the aged ruler in his last moments. The monks sat near-by praying with deep devotion that God guide their beloved king to the highest realms of the Heavens. Outside the marble towers, the king's army had heard the rumor of his immanent passing, and the young buck warriors were already fighting for supremacy and boasting of their personal prowess and lioness strength.

"I'm the best." "I am the strongest." "I deserve to be king." "I will be the next ruler." "Fight me for the throne." Restless echoes of jostling male egos and a surfacing panic created a deep turmoil in the peaceful realm.

"A new beginning must come now. Against our will, our noble king lies dying, and we don't know how to replace him. Finding a monarch as loving and devoted to his people will not be an easy task," said one minister.

As the royal one took one last surrendered breath, the assembled ministers and holy monks knelt in prayer. "Lord, who has given our nation this very righteous leader, do not forsake us for our worldliness or ignorance. We ask that in your Divine mercy you help us to choose our next ruler so that our people might continue in peace and prosperity."

One of the wisest and most trusted of the king's ministers was a mystic named Acara. Clear of avarice and sympathetic to all people, he was the mentor and guide for the younger ones. The king had loved him the most, because he could lean on him heavily for advice. Even the monarch, who had possessed clarity beyond most mortals, knew that one still needs true friends and advisors who speak frankly and cannot be bought.

Acara spent subsequent days and weeks walking the rural market places and busy streets of his country so that he might assess the changing emotions and energy of his people. He prayed continually that he might be guided to a predecessor for the king who would be fearless, brave, and kind. One morning after prayers an unusual intuition came to him. All of nature marks creatures by patterns. The black widow spider's red back is different from the house spider's brown. One is dangerous, the other helpful. One snake is poisonous, the other helps the gardens. One knows this by their markings. If nature makes this so apparent, what of the faces of men? Could there be facial markings that appear consistently in great souls? Facial features that marked a man for a powerful Destiny?

Long and many years had Acara studied the face of his beloved king as he listened to him, advised him, and was his friend. He had lovingly memorized the monarch's every line, crease and feature. The thought came to him that nature herself might show him how to find a man of Destiny if he could remember all the facial features of the monarch and those he had seen in foreign kings and noble statesmen.

And here was the list he wrote:

- Long earlobes, thick and large
- Noble brow, eyebrows round and full
- Large, wide forehead that was clear of blemishes
- Eyes which radiated kindness and nobility
- Full cheeks of rounded softness
- Strong teeth which were evenly spaced
- Large, wide jaw, which was both powerful and fearless
- Balanced lips that naturally upturned at the edges
- Large ears like an elephant
- Mouth that smiled and loved to laugh
- Clear eyes that saw all yet were not petty
- Thick, full hair that shown with radiant health
- Open, upper ear rim that was perfectly shaped
- Large, inner ear hole that allowed sound to enter easily
- Forward chin for bravery

"And so here is what I must look for." Acara put down his pen, "It matters not if this man be a merchant, forest dweller or wealthy prince. These facial features reveal greatness of character. So his background or position in life will not matter. I will keep an open mind that God and nature herself might guide me." And so he stood up, put his water and scanty food into his pack and started his long journey.

Acara walked for days and months meeting and looking at hundreds of men – farmers, merchants, monks, great archers, and cunning warriors. Yet none possessed the facial features from his list. When he had almost given up his quest, a traveler told him of a hut in the woods where there lived a saintly man named Narada. Without stopping to rest or even taken his evening meal Acara directed his footsteps into the forest.

The minister reached the hut quickly and was greeting warmly by the young Narada. Tired but excited from his travels, Acara looked deeply into the face of the young man as he searched for the facial features of Destiny. Mentally he checked them off one by one. Narada had them all. Acara sighed and gave inner thanks that his journey for a new ruler might at last be at an end.

So excited was he that the minister immediately blurted out his request, asking Narada to come rule the country. Unlike others Acara had met who were only too eager to take the throne (but for the wrong reasons), Narada was taken aback by the request. He raised both his hands in the air to push away the offer.

"Honored minister," Narada began, "I know nothing of ruling a kingdom. I am not trained in the art of politics or dealings with nations. I am a simple man – at one with nature. You need a great warrior or a man who has mastery over delicate words to lead your people. I do not possess the skill or power to maneuver those who wish for power, prestige or wealth. I would lose my way and be of little use to our citizens. Ask the Divine One to guide you to one more suited to your needs."

The white-cloaked elder bowed his head before the clear humility of the younger soul. "Narada, we have seen warriors and men of verbal adeptness. Through centuries we have seen them rise and fall, unable to sustain our peoples' love. Our court looks now for a ruler with a pure heart. For we have learned that a king rules as he lives.

We need a man of holiness even if he is untrained in the webs of politics and contract negotiations. For despite the restlessness or worldliness of our people, they know when a monarch loves them. They know when a man is centered in God. For he is just, kind and fair. His calmness in decisions of court goes beyond his emotions or personal opinions. He rules with a generous hand. He holds nothing back from his heart.

"The young ones among us must see this altruism lived out or they will completely forsake the ways of their elders. And the elders, whose bodies have become frail, must see the embodiment of their struggles and dreams carried out by a worthy successor. Our kingdom must be ruled by a man of inner greatness. Again, my lord, I offer you our kingdom to rule. Please do not refuse me. I beg of you." With that Acara put down his staff and sat on the near-by rock.

Narada became quiet and thoughtful as he paced in front of his thatched cottage door. He turned his mind to God and quiet, deep introspection. "Acura, my respected counselor, let me offer you food and drink before we talk of this. Come. Lie down on the cot within my house that you might rest after your long pilgrimage. You must be very weary."

Acura followed Narada into the simple one room dwelling to sleep and rest. Narada put cool cloths on the elder's forehead and gave him the choicest delicacies from the fruit trees. The family of deer outside drew closer to the hut where their friend Narada resided. The forest peacefully rested on into the night, the big and important question of ruling a country absorbed into the sound of crickets and cool stillness of a full moon. Narada lay down on a mat near the bed where his new friend, Acara, lay sleeping. He felt for this old man whose only goal was the safety and protection of his people – a minister whose whole body and life span had been given up in service to guide and inspire the young, the old, the sick, the weak, and even the powerful.

And the young man asked for inner guidance about this issue of ruling a kingdom. In his secret heart he brought to flower the real reason that kept him back from the great honor, which at any juncture might become a great burden. Narada reflected, "What if I lose my way in the myriads of court intrigues, jealousies, or maneuverings? I have no footing to keep me resolute in seeking goodness. What if I lose myself in the outer desires for wealth, power or restless longings? There could be no greater pain to my heart than to lose the inner communion I now feel." With that thought he put his head to his mat and fell asleep.

He rose in the morning to make food for his friend and draw cool water from the well for their baths and refreshments. As he took down the metal pot for brewing the leaves from the trees, a new insight came strongly through his consciousness.

"What have I done to serve my land?" he asked himself, "I am young and strong. Though I am not perfect or trained, I am willing. I am willing to serve and give to the very limits of my physical strength and stamina. At least I can go and make my supreme effort to bring forth good. I will let go of my personal worries about my unworthiness and lack of skill. I will go with an attitude of conquest, service, and willingness to learn."

He prayed out loud in the still air, "Lord, purify my heart that I might serve them in strength."

With his new resolution and heart wide open to his new life, he stepped outside into the forest stillness. As if nature's response was spontaneous and caressing, the talkative birds came to land on his shoulders. They began singing their joyous melodies. The mother and baby deer emerged from behind the bushes to gently lick his hands and to let him stroke the ears of the baby. Even the leopard, which always remained hidden by night and by day, came unabashed before Narada to say good-bye. The brown garden snakes lifted their heads as they approached the quiet hut of their friend. All nature came to love him and wish him well. He knew in his heart that this was God's way of guiding him.

When Acara opened his eyes, Narada was sitting next to him with a banquet of forest delights for the guest's morning nourishment. Fresh coconut juice from the trees, the softest and sweetest of mangoes, calming teas and honey, and perfectly cooked rice and lentils. Acara's worn cloak had been washed and dried by the sunlight. And near Narada's leg was a wooden bowl of special oil so that he might wash and rub the elder's feet before the long journey back to the capitol.

The older minister, who had rarely received such personal service during the course of his travels, was touched and humbled. He said within his heart, "By your actions, Narada, you have shown me that I have chosen the right one to lead our people. Even in the midst of a personal challenge, you have sought only for my comfort, not your own. This will surely forebode well for our nation." And he reached out his sun baked hand to bless Narada's head.

After the morning prayers and food, Narada addressed the older man, "Great sir, I am moved by the offer you made me yesterday to rule the kingdom. I know that my background is unworthy of this honor. However, I am willing. I ask that God give me the Grace to move forward and be a strong, compassionate leader for your people. I ask that you and the other elders guide me through the intricacies of court life as I strive to do my best for you. I will go back with you. If I can be of genuine service to you and our nation, I will stay as long as you need me. If at any time you feel that I have lost my usefulness, please bring me back to this simple hut in the forest. And I will be content."

And with that he packed his sparse belongs into his sack. The birds spread the good news through the trees. Hundreds of curious citizens gathered along the paths to greet the new king. Men held their children above their shoulders so that the little ones might see. Women dropped flowers in front of his feet on the dusty roads to the capitol.

The young Narada ruled wisely for many years. He was just and fair in his court rulings over disputes. He cared nothing for jewels, so he put all the wealth he received back into the farmers' lands and the children's education. The people loved him, and he became a legend as he led them into a time of unparalleled peace and prosperity.

He ruled as he lived.

ABOUT THE AUTHOR

At UCSD School of Medicine Barbara Roberts was co-winner of the Hewing Medical Award for Research, co-publishing abstracts and papers in OB/GYN (NIH). Using her clinical medical background and undergraduate psychological orientation, (Phi Beta Kappa, Magna Cum Laude from Case-Western Reserve), she developed her unique Face Reading system – the only one to honor all ethnic groups, ages, and genders.

In 25 years of private practice presenting over 400 Seminars, she has read more than 10,000 people's faces and appeared on 75 national/local TV Shows: TYRA BANKS, NBC NIGHTLY NEWS, THE YOUNG AND THE RESTLESS (pilot), THE LEARNING CHANNEL, KUSI MORNING NEWS, INSIDE SAN DIEGO, TAMMY FAYE SHOW, and on Daniels, Cox, and Southwestern Cable.

Her first book, *Face Reading: What Does Your Face Say?* (1994) sells internationally. Barbara's Seminars include those for the US Navy, Fortune 500, Wells Fargo, Jenny Craig, UCSD Diversity Conference, UCLA, USD, National University, City of San Diego, The Learning Annex, Hospice, Center for Integrative Medicine, West Coast Nephrology Conference, YMCA, Wellness Center of San Diego, Oasis, MiraCosta and Palomar Colleges, IMS Ready (Surgical Company), San Diego Kiwanis Club.

"Barbara has become perhaps the most effective Face Reader I have encountered in my travels. She is a Face Reader par excellence, and a person of great compassion, sensitivity, and commitment."

– *Dr. Narayan Singh, Author, Face-Reading Expert (Barbara's teacher)*

"Barbara has rare gifts of insight and a wonderful sense of humor. I have found her work helpful in my own life and private practice."

– *Dr. Martha Odegaard, LAC, LaJolla, California*

"The first time I went to Barbara Roberts for a face reading, it was like I was meeting an old friend. Barb started me on my journey to self-awareness. When I am with her I feel a sense of inner peace."

– *Jorge Insua, TV Sr. Supervising Producer, The Christina Show*

Would you like to learn more?

HOW TO GET YOUR OWN
PERSONAL FACE READING

Go to www.facereading1.com.
Look for box "How To Get a Personal Face Reading"

Understand your strengths and areas for personal growth, specific guidance for your emotional, spiritual, and physical healing, increase your self-awareness and personal happiness.

PRIVATE LESSONS WITH BARBARA

Apply Face Reading to your own life by learning how to put all the facial features together. In private phone Lessons, Barbara will guide you through step-by-step analysis of photos. Make this real for you! Become more accurate in how you see and relate to people. Fun and easy to learn!

BARBARA CAN BE REACHED AT 760.479.0008
EMAIL: FACEREADING1@AOL.COM